Insights

on

Leadership

From the
Integral Leadership Review

Volume 2: Developing Leaders

Foreword by

Richard A. Couto, Professor
Antioch University,
PhD Program in Leadership and Change

Russ Volckmann, Editor

Published by the Integral Leadership Review
http://www.integralleadershipreview.com
733 Mermaid Avenue
Pacific Grove, California, USA 93950
831 333-9200

ISBN: 978-0-6151-8094-6

Table of Contents

Foreword

Richard A. Couto

About a year ago, Russ Volckmann wrote me to explain that some of my work suggested that I was an integral leadership theorist. I greeted this news with as much satisfaction as Moliere's character, Monsieur Jourdain. Jourdain was delighted to learn that he had been speaking prose all his life. Not that naïve, I knew there were many more than two ways to study leadership, not just prose or verse; some complain that we have too many ways to do so. Still I was pleased to know of yet another theoretical approach and that there was a name for some of what I did from intuition and tacit beliefs. Having learned that I did integral leadership theory, unlike Jourdain, I set out to find out more about what it is.

Russ and I arranged to have an hour long telephone call in which he explained to me the nature of integral leadership theory. I certainly liked what I heard—individual and social human systems and the interrelationship of their development, complexity theory, but most of all the integration of the work of a set of writers about whom I was hoping to learn more. Several students had introduced me already to Ken Wilber, the Shambhala Institute, *Presence,* and related work and authors. Russ has been an excellent guide introducing me to the work of Don Beck, Christopher Cohen, Clare Graves, and Jenny Wade as well as to people, such as Sara Nora Ross, who introduced me to the work of many others contributing to integral leadership theory. Soon, I began finding integral leadership theory where I had not seen it before and in talking with people, I learned many others had preceded me in the discovery of this interesting set of ideas or related ones. I felt like Monsieur Jourdain again knowing now that I spoke and thought in a language shared by many others. Russ invited me to a portal of an exciting world of big questions and earnest, insightful ways to address them.

This publication offers you a similar invitation. If you are coming to integral leadership theory for the first time, you are in for a genuine treat. If you are already familiar with this work, you already know the quality of Russ's insightful interviews with thoughtful people, some of whom, like me, did not know they were integral leadership theorists. Russ is building a much needed movement to develop valuable intellectual, teaching, and action networks. He provides a hub to the human spokes in that movement, such as the people in this issue who question the inevitability of the unsatisfactory and inadequate present state of affairs and suggest effective and humane alternatives. You will find in these pages a delightful combination of a scholarship of discovery and of synthesis; insights into the way things work; ideas about how they might work better; and interpretations of the related ideas of other thinkers.

Volume 2 of *Insights on Leadership* compiles interviews from the *Integral Leadership Review* with Raine Eisler, Fred Kofman, Susanne Cook-Greuter, Leo Burke, and William R. Torbert. Russ's interaction with each of them explores central questions of human purpose of individuals and groups—families, communities, organizations, nations, and global society—and their dynamic relationships. I found connections to leadership literature with which I was familiar—James MacGregor Burns, Howard Gardner, Robert Greenleaf, Ronald Heifetz, Jean Lipman-Blumen, and Margaret Wheatley; validation for my own approaches to leadership praxis such as action research and personal competencies; parallels with social scientists whose work puts the study of leadership studies in a much larger context—especially the early and phenomenological work of Karl Marx, the efforts of Emile Durkheim to ground individual actions in the differences among social groups, and Gunnar Myrdal and Kurt Lewin's forays into field theory; and more insight into the set of thinkers to whom Russ had introduced me. Fred Kofman's interview offers wonderful insights into Ken Wilber's work in particular.

While it is clear that integral theory has many contributing streams of thought, it is not merely their confluence. As Russ explains, this volume is "about surfacing ideas and perspectives that will help us build an integral theory of leadership." As in my case, Russ finds integral thinkers in each of the people interviewed here, even if they are unfamiliar with integral theory. What emerges from the words on these pages is an approach to integrating theories of leadership with awareness that behavior and development have correlates to the interior states of individuals, to culture and to systems.

My manuscript text has marginal notes and underlining throughout suggesting the numerous insights that I gained: dominator and partnership models with their correlates to the forms of power from *power over* to *power within*; the utility of archetypes of gender and of heroes in understanding and explaining leadership; the swamp land of fear which undermines efforts to construct hierarchies of actualization; the difference of members and parts of a social system; the different strategies entailed in incorporating people and groups, at different levels of development, in joint efforts whether it is going on a holiday or pursuing lofty values; the importance of horizontal development at any stage and the inherent contradiction of working to "achieve" a higher stage of development; the personal elements of leadership such as compassion and awareness; the skills of leadership such as listening; the many facets of spirituality and their relevance for leadership; empowering as "the exercise of power in an appropriately vulnerable, mutuality-enhancing, transforming way"; and the role of action logic, research, and theatre to create genuine learning organizations and communities.

More than anything else, I left these pages with insights into some wonderful work on leadership and a sense of the importance for me to look into them further. When you leave these pages, I hope you will have gained as many and as good insights as I did. Also, I hope that you will have your own reason for thanking Russ Volckmann for this book and all his other work of which it is a part.

Richard A. Couto is a founding faculty member of the Antioch University PhD program in Leadership and Change,. In 1991, he became a founding faculty member of the Jepson School of Leadership Studies at the University of Richmond; the world's first such undergraduate school. His most recent books focus on community leadership, democratic theory and practice and a curriculum of courage for higher education.

He recently published **Reflections on Leadership**, commemorating the 25th anniversary of James MacGregor Burns's book, **Leadership**. He is also meeting with a group, directed by Burns, on a general theory of leadership and has a chapter in **The Question for a General Theory of Leadership,** edited by Georgia Sorenson. He has entered fields of inquiry new to him—terrorism and political leadership, creativity, leadership competencies in the political sector, and sacred texts and leadership.

Introduction to Volume 2

The *Integral Leadership Review* has published excerpts and complete interviews over the last few years with leading practitioners, developers and theorists of leadership. We have called this series "Fresh Perspectives," because each of the people we have interviewed has something fresh and important to say about the subject of leadership. This series of publications drawn from these interviews we have titled Insights on Leadership, because we believe they offer to anyone interested in the subject of leadership a way of understanding the perspectives and experiences of those with significant innovative approaches related to leadership. In this second volume, we provide interviews with five leading thinkers about leadership who are each involved in developing leaders:

Leo Burke

Susanne Cook-Greuter

Riane Eisler

Fred Kofman

William R. Torbert

Each of these writers has made a significant impact on the practice, development and study of leadership Their work has attracted interest in the domains of business, government and education. .

Leo Burke led Motorola's leadership development program before going to the University of Notre Dame as Associate Dean and Director of Executive Education. His concerns are practicality and relevance to the world of business. He developed a one-week program in Integral Leadership that has attracted hundreds of executives in the last few years. Evaluation results are overwhelmingly positive. Leo has been ranked 5.0 out of a possible 5.0 for overall quality of his teaching by his students.

He has also participated in Integral Organizational Leadership programs for the Integral Institute in Boulder, Colorado.

Susanne Cook-Greuter is an amazing scholar. From Switzerland, she went to Washington University in St. Louis, Missouri and studied with developmetnal psychologist, Jane Loevinger. Subsequently, she spent 15 years collecting data, prior to going to Harvard to complete her PhD. In the meanwhile, she has developed the Leadership Development Profile that provides feedback on stages of development. This profile has been used by her, Bill Torbert and others in working with leadership development and research. Susanne has published *Creativity, Spirituality, and Transcendence: Paths to Integrity and Wisdom in the Mature Self*, and *Transcendence and Mature Thought in Adulthood*, each with co-author Melvin E. Miller. She, is active in programs on leadership at the Integral Institute in Boulder, Colorado and is a member of the Integral Leadership Council for the *Integral Leadership Review*.

Riane Eisler is probably the most widely read author in this volume. Her *Chalice and the Blade* is an international best seller. Among her other works is *The Real Wealth of Nations: Creating a Caring Economics*. She is the President and founder of the Center for Partnership Studies. She is co-founder of the SpiritualAlliance to Stop Intimate Violence. Her writing on leadership has appeared in a number of publications, including *Leadership is Global: Co-Creating a More Humane and Sustainable World*, edited by Walter Link, Thais Corral and Mark Gerzon. She was born in Vienna, Austria; she and her family fled the Nazis and came to the United States after several years in Cuba.

Fred Kofman is certainly the person most intimate with the thinking of Ken Wilber, the leading

American philosopher who has contributed so much to the development of integral theory. He and Ken have been neighbors for a number of years after Fred moved to Boulder from Cambridge, Massachusetts where he taught at M.I.T. He worked closely there with Peter Senge and was a founding member of the Society for Organizational Learning. Fred is originally from Argentina and most of his writing is in Spanish. However, he has published **Conscious Business: How to Build Value Through Values**. His CD set on Conscious Business is also an important contribution to leadership development.

William R. Torbert, author and teacher, consultant and artist in his own right, has worked with Susanne Cook-Greuter and others in the application of integral and transformational concepts in leadership and organizations. His most recent book, with several contributors, is **Action Inquiry**. After teaching at Yale, SMU, and Harvard, Bill has been at Boston College for the past 25 years, serving as Graduate Dean of the School of Management for 9 years and Director of the PhD program in Organizational Transformation. Among his other books are **Personal and Organisational Transformations: Through Action inquiry** and **Sources of Excellence**. Bill is a member of the Integral Leadership Council for the **Integral Leadership Review**.

All Interviews in this volume were conducted by Russ Volckmann, founder and editor of the **Integral Leadership Review**. He was an organization development consultant for 22 years and an executive coach since 1997. He has authored numerous articles, an ebook—**A Leadership Opportunity**—and **1 Phoenix Rising**.

The perspective used in conducting these conversations:

We hold an assumption that it is not only possible to find an approach to integrating theories of leadership, but that we have found an approach with considerable potential for doing so. This approach is known as integral theory. It has many antecedents, however the most current and prolific writings on integral theory have been done by the American philosopher, Ken Wilber. The essence of this approach is that every occurrence, or leadership event in our area of interest, contains four elements: what is interior to the individual, individual behaviors, culture and systems. There is a map of these provided on page 71 of this publication. In addition, development is seen as occurring in stages and along multiple lines of development. However, as you read these pages it will be useful for you to keep in mind several concepts that are at the heart of Ken Wilber's integral theory.

Please refer to the notes for an explanation of the All Quadrant All Levels framework. The point is that every occurence can be viewed as having variables located in all four quadrants of what Wilber calls a holon (after the work of xxxxx); a holon is something that can be understood as both a whole unto itself and a part of something else. An example of this in biology would be a cell, which we can treat as an independent unit of analysis, yet it is also a component of a more complex organism such as an amoeba or an organ in the human body. Thus, the use of holons in a hierarchy is a holarchy, based on variances in complexity and capacity. The four cell matrix is a tool for mapping these variables in any occurence.

Another variable in Wilber's model include is the stage of development in a holarchy. Therefore, there is a strong affinity in the relationship between integral theory and developmental psychology. The interviews to follow are replete with examples of this.

An additional variable is called streams or lines. This relates closely to Howard Gardner's notion of multiple intelligences. Examples of streams would be cognitive, emotional, spiritual, kinesthetic, relationship and so on. This is an important variable in thinking about leadership, because we can recognize variances in the exercise of leadership by understanding the different levels of development of individuals along each of these streams.

8

Style constitutes still another variable. Here we find such factors as masculine and feminine or the styles associated with Carl Jung's theory of personality as represented in the Myers-Briggs Typology Inventory. The degree to which we can incorporate the idea of "leadership styles" has not been addressed yet in the literature.

Finally, states is a variable contrasted with stages. While stages tend to be more longlasting and difficult to change, states are brief experiences. An example might be an altered state of consciousness or a state of confusion. If you are experiencing any of that at this moment, you will get greater clarity as you read the interviews.

There is a very close relationship between integral theory and developmental psychology since both are concerned with stages of development. Major theorists that have been cited most frequently in integral theory are Robert Kegan, Jane Loevinger and her work as further developed by Susanne Cook-Greuter, Clare Graves (as represented in the work of Don Beck and Chris Cowan in Spiral Dynamics®) and Jenny Wade. This does not mean that other theorists or approaches to psychology are excluded. It is a fundamental principle of integral theory that all approaches, all theories hold some truth to be included.

Criticisms and extensions of the integral work of Ken Wilber and other integral theorists can be found in a number of books and online websites. The latter include Frank Visser's wonderful website, http://www.worldofintegral.net, and a peer reviewed online journal, http://www.integral-review.org, as well as http://www.integralleadershipreview.com.

There is much to be developed in integral theory. It is a work in progress. For example, the idea of lines of development relates to the work of Howard Gardner on multiple intelligences and Daniel Goleman, Richard Boyatzis and others on emotional intelligence. In integral theory, typical lines of development (and there are many more) include emotional, cognitive, relationship, physical, kinesthetic, and spiritual. We can see how all of these (and more) would have relevance for the study of leadership. Thus, when we think of training, educating and developing individuals for leadership roles, their development along all of these lines would be integrally important. Imbalances result in ineffective leadership. One of the areas yet to be fully developed in integral theory includes ideas about lines of development for cultures and systems, although Spiral Dynamics® (see Page 71) offers considerable insight on this and further approaches include the work of Isaak Adizes on corporate life cycles..

Thus, the explorations in this and other volumes in this series are about surfacing ideas and perspectives that will help us build an integral theory of leadership. Some of the people interviewed are very familiar with integral theory, some are not. But they are all integral thinkers, as I think you will see as you read their comments.

—*Russ Volckmann, PhD*

Partnership and Leadership
Riane Eisler

Introduction with Mike McElhenie

You can read about Riane Eisler in the interview. However, before you read the interview with her, you may find the following material to be interesting and in harmony with much of what Riane talked about in our conversation. I spoke with Michael McElhenie, one of the leaders of the "Leadership for Results" United Nations program that helps catalyze collaborative solutions to HIV/AIDS in Africa, SE Asia and the Caribbean. This is something he had to say that is very relevant to the interview.

Mike: We started these programs in 2001; we saw results right off the bat. What we were doing was trying to impact multiple levels of systems. We wanted to impact individuals intrapsychically and behaviorally—to change how they saw themselves, how they saw their worlds and how they took action in them. We wanted to impact relationships throughout vast interconnected networks. Most importantly, we wanted these leaders to develop and implement more collaborative, more complete solutions to the complex issues surrounding HIV and AIDS. So when we talk about results we are talking about results at many levels of systems.

Russ: I remember one story you told (Integral Leadership in Action conference, Westminster, Colorado, April 2005) about bringing men and women into separate and then mixed groups to talk about their gender and sexual relationships and the impact that had. It brought tears to my eyes.

Mike: This work was tremendous! One of the things that is very clear in the research cited by our friends at the United Nations Development

Program is that when you increase women's empowerment you decrease the incidence of HIV and AIDS.

Russ: What you are saying is so in keeping with the message that Riane Eisler is putting forth.

Mike: Yes, it is absolutely true and I see this reflected in Riane's writing. We are seeing it on a small scale and a large scale. It has been particularly true in Cambodia. Gretchen Schmelzer and Fran Johnston have been integral in the work there. Along with efforts to increase the power and the visibility of women, we have seen a significant decrease in the incidence of HIV and AIDS and, in particular, the stigma related to HIV and AIDS. Increasing the voice of women helps everyone, including men, bring their compassionate energy into the various systems in which they are involved, whether it is at the societal level or more local. This increases people's awareness of how their maltreatment of others, particularly those living with HIV/AIDS, is not creating a better society. So women's empowerment is an incredibly important variable not only in addressing HIV and AIDS, but also in improving the general health and wellbeing of society.

In the story you mentioned, men and women first met as gender groups in separate rooms and talked about what it meant to be a man or a woman. What it meant to be a good or bad man. What it meant to be a good or bad woman. They talked about all of their experiences related to that. For the men I was with, they slowly and quite cautiously began to admit to each other— after some people in power spoke up first— that having a woman initiate sex feels good. It does a lot for the ego and it does a lot for the relationship. That was an acknowledgement by the men in this room, for the first time in their collective history, that women actually enjoyed intimate relationships.

Some would say, "You're kidding me! How could this possibly be so?" Yet, the denial began to break down, led by the powerful men in the group, and men began opening themselves up to another reality regarding this important aspect of gender relationships.

What this opening up did at a psychological and a social level was to level the playing field just a bit and men, and the women they shared this new insight with, said, "Wow! We are in this together!" It is not just men holding the power and being the authority over everything. It is being partners and we are not that different and, at the same time, our differences are subtler. People can embrace both sides of that reality and be able to move forward in their relationships in a different way.

In one workshop, a very powerful policeman from Swaziland was brought to tears at the realization that he had been ignoring the needs of his wife for twenty some odd years. He decided to have a discussion with her about this insight that very night. The next day he came and his wife was right next to him. As I

was to lead the group that day, she came up to me and said, "Michael, I wanted to come in and see what had so powerfully moved my husband to want to be my partner, not just my husband."

I swear, you talked about stories bringing tears to your eyes, well that was what was happening right there in front of 50 people. My partner doing the workshop with me, Felice Tilin, saw me hugging this woman and her husband and all of us letting loose these joyful tears. She came up with tears in her own eyes and asked, "What's going on?" I said, "We are just having a wonderful moment." She said, "I felt it from across the room."

And now, Riane Eisler:

RV: A way to begin this would be to help the readers have a sense of who you are and what you've been about in your career.

RE: I sometimes have said that my life is like the pieces of a jigsaw puzzle coming together, because I have a varied background.

"in the 60's, like many women, I suddenly realized that as important as having been born Jewish had been in my life, having been born female probably affected my life even more."

I have a background academically in both sociology and in law. I have used that background to embark on what my work has been: a systems study of our past, present and the possibilities for our future as a species. That is fairly big, right? My first job was as a systems scientist at the Systems Development Corporation, an offshoot of the Rand Corporation. Already in the 50's, when nobody talked about systems, that was something that I was involved in.

Perhaps the most significant parts of my background are two-fold. One was what happened when I was a child and the Nazis took over my native Austria. That was cataclysmic for me, of course. We had to flee and it completely changed my life. It brought up the question that my work sought to answer: when we have such an enormous capacity for caring, for empathy, for creativity and yes, for love, why is it that there has been so much cruelty, so much violence, so much destructiveness? Is it inevitable—as we are often told—or do we have alternatives? That is a burning question for many of us. It certainly was for me starting very early in my life.

The second formative experience was not only the immigration process, the changing of so many cultures—first to Cuba, then later to the United States—but in the 60's, like many women, I suddenly realized that as important as having been born Jewish had been in my life, having been born female probably affected my life even more. As happened with many women at that time—I realized that many problems that I had thought were personal were really cultural and social. That was very important because one of the things that distinguish my research methodology is that most studies of human society are quite aptly called the study of man. And then we are told, "Don't worry, man includes woman." Well actually, woman includes man...

(Laughter)

RE: ...but the point of it is that these studies use a very, very incomplete database. Not only that, but when you focus on one half of humanity, you don't take into full account the domain that is primarily associated with women, namely, family and other intimate relations. In other words, the private rather than the so-called public sphere is ignored. So in my research, I was able to see patterns and configurations that are not visible otherwise,

because I drew from a much larger database.

There were no names for these configurations. Connecting the dots was what was possible at that point, because if we only look at part of the picture, we don't see the configuration of the whole picture, right? So there were no names and I had to name them. I named one configuration the dominator or domination model and the other one the partnership model. I also use the term "gylanic," because the cultural construction of the relationship of the roles of the two halves of humanity is a key element of the social system.

RV: Your partnership model and dominator model concepts are very interesting, because they aren't just about interpersonal relationships or family relationships, but they are also about social, economic and political relationships, as well.

RE: They are about everything, really. The whole picture includes women, children and early childhood relations, which are so foundational to a society, and affect everything. We're socialized to just sort of immediately ghetto-ize that and say, "Oh, this is about women and children," whereas nothing could be further from the truth. To understand human society we need an approach that takes into account the whole of the population: men, women, and children.

The Dominator Model

RV: Please summarize the quality or characteristics of a dominator model.

RE: We're all very familiar with the characteristics. Basically we're talking about a system of beliefs and a way of structuring institutions—family, education, religion, politics, and economics—in a way that imposes and maintains top-down rankings of domination. I call this a "Hierarchy of

Domination," be it in the family, the state or tribe. And of course, we see it in economics, religion, and education. The partnership and dominator models are just that—models—so we're always talking about the degree to which a particular culture, economic system, business or family orients to one or the other. And these categories go beyond conventional ones such as right vs. left, religious versus secular, or Eastern vs. Western. Examples of rigid dominator cultures are Nazi Germany (a secular Western rightist society), Khomeini's Iran (a religious Eastern society), Stalin's Soviet Union (a leftist society).

> *"The partnership and dominator models are just that—models—so we're always talking about the degree to which a particular culture, economic system, business or family orients to one or the other."*

RV: I was noticing in the paper this morning there was a photograph of a long table with the men who are in the process of trying to forge a constitution in Iraq seated around it. The absence of women is so noticeable.

RE: It is noticeable to us now, and yet I remember in the 60's when I woke up as if from a long sleep this was a problem nobody was talking about. It had been pushed into the background. In those days you picked up a newspaper and 99.9% of the names and faces in the United States were male. Now, we've moved a little from that. But, of course what we're seeing in Iraq now is the takeover of fundamentalism. Whether it's Muslim, Christian or whatever, it is really not a matter of religion. It's a matter of a return to a rigid domination model.

The domination model is a system of top-down rankings. In fundamentalism we see theocratic top-down rule and the ranking of the male half of humanity over the female half. There is also a high degree of built-in, culturally condoned abuse and violence, from very punitive childrearing to "holy wars," and a belief system that presents all that as either divinely ordained or ordained by nature.

RV: So then most of us are very familiar with the dominator model. We've been living in it.

RE: That is a good point because the mere fact that we are having this conversation, of course, shows that we've also begun to move away from it. Consider the European Middle Ages. They looked a lot like the Taliban, didn't they?—the Inquisition, the Crusades, the witch burnings, enormous abuse and violence in child rearing and, of course, chronic, chronic wars and very rigid male dominance.

The Partnership Model

RV: You have an alternative that you suggested as a result of your work and that is a partnership model.

RE: It is so very important that we know that there is an alternative. Just for starters, I would like to say that this alternative is about a configuration. When I use the term partnership, this is not about just strategic alliances or cooperation. People collaborate and cooperate in the domination model. The 9/11 terrorists did; invading armies and monopolies do, etc. So the difference between competition and cooperation isn't the difference between these two models. The difference is that each has a very different cultural configuration.

We can see the partnership configuration in tribal societies such as the Teduray of the Philippines and the Minangkabau of Sumatra. We see it in very technologically developed cultures such as the Nordic cultures: Sweden,

Finland, and Norway. There we see a much closer orientation to the partnership model than anywhere else in the world today, except for tribal islands of earlier cultures.

RV: Would you characterize the partnership model?

RE: Well, let's look at the Nordic Nations. First of all, rather than having hierarchies of domination—these rigid rankings—they do have hierarchies. They have more of what I call hierarchies of actualization. I'll get back to that because it's key to my model for business and economics. But the first thing that you see is that they have much greater political and economic democracy. They don't have these huge gaps betweens haves and have-nots. They have a generally high standard of living for everyone.

Second, rather than ranking of the male half of humanity over the female half, they have much more equal partnership between women and men. With this—and this is critical—you find that as the status of women rises, so does the status of those traits and activities stereotypically considered feminine: caring, care-giving, non-violence.

So what do you see? You see that the Nordic nations were pioneers in what my friend from Finland, Hilkka Pietila, calls a caring society. We call it a welfare state, but it's very different from the U.S. welfare system. They have universal health care, childcare allowances, elder care and paid parental leave. In other words, in cultures that orient to the partnership model, the care giving that is stereotypically associated with women can become a fiscal priority of the nation.

This is very, very good for the economic health of the nation. Finland, for example, in both 2003 and 2004 ranked ahead of the much wealthier, much more powerful United States in the World Economic Forum's Global Competitiveness ratings. And of course, these nations are always on the top in the U.N. Human Development Reports.

These nations also pioneered the first peace studies courses. They pioneered laws against physical punishment of children in families. They pioneered a strong men's movement to disentangle male identity from violence. They also pioneered what we today call industrial democracy, teamwork in factories, rather than turning human beings into mere cogs in the industrial machine. Ecologically sound manufacturing, such as the Natural Step, was also pioneered by them.

Now, none of this is random or coincidental. It's part of the cultural configuration characteristic of the partnership rather than domination model. It is a configuration that factors both what happens to the female half of humanity and also what happens in people's day-to-day lives.

RV: In addition to **The Chalice and The Blade**, you wrote a book with David Loye, your husband, called, **The Power of Partnership**, in which you were trying to help people learn how to make the shift from a dominator orientation to a partnership orientation. Is that correct?

RE: That's right. The first book that came out of my cross-cultural, historical, multidisciplinary study was **The Chalice and The Blade**. Then I wrote another book, Sacred Pleasure, which looks at the cultural construction of both sexuality and spirituality using the analytical lens of the partnership-domination continuum. My next two books were very much concerned with putting all this into action. I wrote a book, Tomorrow's Children, on applying my findings to partnership education.

Then came my last published book, **The**

Power of Partnership. That was a real departure for me. I decided to do this in the form of a self-help book. As a matter of fact, it won the Nautilus Award as the best self-help book of 2003. However, it's a very different genre of self-help book. Most self-help books talk about how we relate to ourselves, our intimate relations and our work relations. But this book goes on to our community and national relations, to our international relations, to our relations with Mother Earth and yes, our spiritual relations, showing how they are all interconnected and—even beyond that—how very different every one of these relations is depending on the degree to which there is an orientation to the partnership model or the domination model. That book is an action book. It is full of action checklists. It's a how-to book.

Lines and Development

RV: It is. There are many activities on all the different levels or in the different lines that you were just talking about. As I heard you describing that, what came to mind was in integral theory, the notion of lines: that we have multiple lines of development. Intellectual might be one, emotional another. Certainly how we engage in relationships is one. There are many different ways that lines of development could be described or characterized. What strikes me about **The Power of Partnership** and all your work on **The Partnership Way**, is that you're doing what the Integral approach is talking about: development along multiple lines, whether it has to do with self, relationship or community.

RE: Very true. I would say that certainly from the perspective of the new conceptual framework of the partnership/domination continuum, we cannot really develop fully in any area, whether it is emotionally, spiritually or mentally, under the domination model. For one thing, it is a very stressful model and stress gets in the way of full development, because our brain's neurochemistry tends to go into fight, flight or disassociation. The difference with my work is that my focus is on the conditions that we need to put in place—and that we can put in place—so that we can more fully develop, so that we can live in a culture that supports, rather than inhibits the full development of our enormous capacities, which really are so striking in humans: our capacities for consciousness, for caring, for creativity.

RV: Riane, as you are probably aware, there are a number of developmental models afloat saying that there are stages in adult development and/or stages in cultural development that suggest that people who are at "lower stages of development" may or may not have developed the cognitive capability, the world view, the values to be able to develop in this way. What you're talking about is really something that is going to be of greater interest to people who are at higher levels of development. If that's the case, that's where it seems to me your more community oriented, collectively oriented aspects become relevant because you're really talking about needing to change culture and individuals.

"In a hierarchy of actualization, you have respect, benefit and accountability flowing both ways."

RE: That's the whole point. It's really a chicken and egg issue, isn't it? We have individual responsibility. But as I show again and again in **The Power of Partnership**, if we don't change the culture, change will be inhibited. We hear so much about healing. But we are trying to heal ourselves in a dominator cultural context. It's like trying to go up in a down elevator.

We must work through our own dominator

mental and emotional tapes that run. We have inherited them. Our parents didn't invent them. They inherited them, etc., etc. The fact that they are much weaker now is a very good sign, even though we are in a time of regression when there are those who are trying to make them much stronger again.

Not coincidentally, these people are focusing on the primary human relations between women and men and parents and children. They intuitively recognize that these relations are foundational—while sadly most progressives still tend to see them as "just" women and children's issues.

Our job is awareness and then action. The more we change our cultural environment, the more we can also have more awareness. And then we are also more able to act.

But I would say this: it isn't just cognitive development that's the issue. This is a difference between my approach and that of many of the stage models that people have become so interested in. It's emotional. It's very important that we become aware that emotional development or lack of it impacts cognitive development.

People who were brought up in a very rigid dominator way, unless they are exposed to alternatives—including but not necessarily therapy—tend to see only two alternatives: you dominate or you are dominated. They don't see a partnership alternative.

It's our job—and I've certainly taken it upon myself as part of my job—to show everyone that not only is a partnership alternative possible, but that it is much more effective economically and, of course, much more equitable, pleasurable, and far less stressful. As many of us are aware, today the mix of high technology, nuclear bombs, biological terrorism, conquest of nature with ever more

powerful technologies possibly will take us to an evolutionary dead end. We urgently need a cultural transformation and that's our job.

RV: Ultimately, I want to get to the question of leadership, but I think there is still more foundation to be laid. For example, you brought up the subject of economics. In a new book that's coming out called **Enlightened Power** yours is the first chapter: "The Economics of the Enlightened Use of Power." Can you lay out for us a little bit of the economic argument in support of a partnership approach?

RE: It is something I'm very deeply involved in. I am actually working on a new book on partnership economics: a caring economy. We've been told for a long time, for example in terms of organizational structure, that hierarchies of domination are needed for success. In these hierarchies of rigid top down rankings, accountability, respect, and benefit flow mostly from the bottom up. Enron, for example, certainly didn't have much accountability or respect from the top down. Most of the benefits accrued to the people on top. That's the classic domination model. And Enron shows that in the long term it's hardly successful.

I don't mean to pick on Enron. But these hierarchies of domination, where there is so little accountability or respect by those on top, are rife with horrible corruption and cause great suffering and loss. These companies eventually went bankrupt or changed their names. These were disasters for many people: stockholders, employees and their pension plans. What we're discovering today—and it's all over the management literature—is that hierarchies of actualization are much more efficient, much more effective.

Now what is a hierarchy of actualization? Well, if we look at the way power is conceptualized, it isn't conceptualized so much as power over, power to dominate or to destroy, but power to empower oneself and others to be the best we can be. It is also power with. So a term like teamwork is really part of the shift to partnership where there's a different way of looking at power.

In a hierarchy of actualization, you have respect, benefit and accountability flowing both ways. But you also have something else that is very important: you have much better information flow. This is very important for companies to make effective business decisions. In partnership structures, not only do you have teamwork where people can really have input and use their brains and their creativity, but you also have the possibility for much more creativity.

When people are in a hierarchy of domination, they know very well that they better conform. It's very dangerous to disobey orders or to question. Particularly in a post-industrial economy where we are told we need a flexible workforce, a creative workforce, a workforce that can solve problems, the hierarchy of domination just does not work. The structure inhibits creativity and flexibility.

"The guru is really a dominator phenomenon. We all need leaders, but we certainly don't need to have leaders who consider it their function to make followers out of us."

There is something else really basic that takes us back to what I was talking about when I spoke of the Nordic Nations. There are many studies now showing that when people feel cared for—which is part of the hierarchy of actualization—people perform much better. There are empirical studies showing this. So all in all, what we're finding out is that the partnership model is not only more conducive to higher stages of human development, but it actually is much more conducive to economic

well-being.

RV: Have you actually been exploring studies to that effect?

RE: Yes, all this will be in my book on caring economics. But I have an article that will be out in a book that is being published by Stanford University that was put together by the people in the Weatherhead School of Management at Case Western Reserve University.

RV: You mean Cooperrider and others?

RE: Yes, David Cooperrider is one of the editors. I was very honored that Case Western Reserve University gave me an honorary Ph.D. in May of this year. I was one of two; the other was the vice president of Uganda.

RV: Congratulations!

RE: It was lovely.

My article is the first chapter in the book, because it frames the rest of the material in the book. It's called, "The Economic Imperative of Revisioning the Rules of the Game: Work, Work Values and Caring." I cite some of those studies. People like Jane Dutton at the University of Michigan have done some of this work. Alice Isen has done a lot of studies on people doing better when they feel better. And of course, people don't feel good in hierarchies of domination. When people feel good, they even negotiate better. It all makes sense.

RV: You carried this theme over into the chapter in *Enlightened Power: The Economics of the Enlightened Use of Power.*

RE: Yes.

Leadership

RV: Let's see if we can talk a little bit about what are the implications of all this for leadership? Some of it may be fairly obvious. Dominator models of leadership are prevalent in most societies. For example, I was doing an interview with someone recently and asked about his definition of leadership and he said a leader is someone who has followers.

(Laughter)

RE: You see, that is a dominator definition.

I do want to say something: we all need teachers, but we don't need gurus. The guru is really a dominator phenomenon. We all need leaders, but we certainly don't need to have leaders who consider it their function to make followers out of us.

RV: So if we don't have followers in a partnership model, what is leadership?

RE: Leadership is many things. First of all it is the capacity to inspire. Second, it is the capacity to have a vision of what one's goals are and how to implement them.

RV: A course of action?

RE: Yes. You see a lot of this in the corporate literature today where you read about the leader and the manager no longer being a cop or a controller, but rather being someone who facilitates. I think the good leader nurtures. That is a statement that takes us back to an important issue: the stereotypically feminine and the stereotypically masculine.

RV: Please tell us about that.

RE: I think that if we really are serious about changing our economic system, about changing our world so that our children and generations still to come will survive and thrive, we need to pay attention to what I call the hidden system of gender values. The sociologist, Louis Wirth, once said that the most important things about a society are those that are seldom talked about. I paraphrase that into "the most important things about a society are those that people feel uncomfortable talking about."

RV: Interesting. Be aware of the shadow.

RE: Well, I'm not a Jungian. I should make that clear. I don't know about shadows. But I do know that if we are uncomfortable talking about gender, if we are uncomfortable talking about parent-child relations as fundamental, as being indexes of social structures and values—which they are—there is a reason for it. We've been so indoctrinated to think that a male superior, female inferior divided species model is either divinely or naturally ordained that we're uncomfortable when it's questioned. That is part of our mental maps, our emotional maps. Yet, if we don't examine that hidden system of gender valuations, we really cannot make the changes that we need for the cultural transformation that so many of us want.

I want to emphasize that we are talking about stereotypes, not anything inherent in women or men. But in the domination model not only women, but also so-called feminine values, such as caring, compassion, empathy and non-violence, are relegated to a secondary subservient place. So we have very strange fiscal priorities. We're told there is no money. But there is always enough money for building prisons and, if you think of it, that's for the dominator archetype of the punitive father, right? And we always have enough money for weapons and wars, and of course that relates to the dominator "masculine" archetype of the warrior.

RV: I thought you said you weren't a Jungian?

(Laughter)

RE: I'm not a Jungian. Let's not even go there because Jung really takes these archetypes as universals rather than as constructs of the domination model. So the archetype of the punitive father is a dominator archetype. It's not a human archetype; fathers don't have to be punitive. But in the domination model, there is always money for punishing; there is always money for wars. Of course, that's another dominator archetype: the hero as violent warrior. This cultural construction of masculinity and its elevation of men over women really governs our systems of values unconsciously. So we're told there is not enough money for what? For the work of caring and care giving, for health care, for child care, for elder care, are you following what I'm saying?

RV: Yes, for education...

RE: In other words, for these "soft", stereotypically feminine things.

If you look at the Nordic Nations, you see a very different set of priorities. These nations were dirt poor at the beginning of the 20th Century. Do you remember the mass immigrations from there, the potato famines, etc.? But when they started to invest in care giving, they became prosperous. And this happened as the status of women rose and policies were instituted with women as half of the legislature there, not just 10-12% like here. They really developed what we so need. They developed high quality human capital that we hear so much about today. So the dominator model is economically a very pernicious system. It is also a system that artificially creates scarcity.

RV: Because it allocates resources in some ways to the exclusions of others?

RE: Absolutely! And it also destroys resources through constant wars and through diverting more and more resources into weaponry. As the weapons get more technologically complex and expensive, it is basically a disaster for the world. And the domination model not only creates material scarcity through misallocation of resources, it also creates emotional scarcity, because if the only alternatives are dominating or being dominated how can you really have intimacy? How can you fulfill that emotional need? It also promotes spiritual scarcity because there's something really immoral about the whole system.

Leadership Today

RV: What is the role of leadership in our current circumstances?

RE: I would like to see leaders world-wide stop thinking in terms of the conventional categories of right versus left, religious versus secular, capitalist versus communist, east versus west, north versus south, technologically developed or underdeveloped. I would like them to think in holistic ways, which is only possible once we transcend this hidden system of gendered valuation.

All these conventional social categories fail to take into account the social and cultural construction of the roles and relations of the two halves of humanity. Why? Because women are so devalued that anything concerning them is not considered important.

"We cannot dismantle the top of the domination pyramid and still leave it's foundations of domination and violence in the primary human relations between women and men and between parents and children largely in place."

I would like to see leaders use the analytical lens of the partnership and domination models, because then they will really see the whole picture. They can make more sound policy decisions. That's the first thing. There is an urgent need for partnership leaders, for leaders that can offer people—whether it's in an organization or in a nation—a vision of a viable and positive alternative and how to get there.

RV: How do you think we need to go about trying to increase the kind of leadership you're talking about in the world and in our organizations?

RE: First of all, I think the challenge for leaders is enormous. For me a leader is somebody who has the spiritual courage to step out of the prevailing paradigm. We're beginning to see partnership leaders all over the world. Wangari Mathaai with her greenbelt movement in Kenya is an example of leadership that empowers. In Brazil, Thais Corral has used radio as a tool to empower women. Now there is a network of 400 women's radio programs that have developed.

Women and Leadership

RV: By implication, are the examples and the strategy for creating more of a partnership approach to leadership focused on women?

RE: Raising the status of women is not going to solve all of our problems, but without it our problems cannot be solved. That is one of the core findings from my work. If you go back to what we were talking about—the shift to a more stereotypically feminine style of leadership that's empowering rather than disempowering, nurturing rather than coercive—we're talking about a hidden gendered system of values becoming embodied in leadership. I want to again emphasize this; this has nothing to do with anything inherent in women or men. Some women can be very cruel and some men can be very caring. And please, bring out that it has a lot to do with the way that the domination model is structured and the way

the partnership model is structured.

We need to—as leaders—now I'm talking socially—observe what the people pushing us back focus on. Whether it was Hitler in Germany, Khomeini in Iran, the fundamentalist alliance in the United States or the so called Muslim Fundamentalists, one of their top priorities is always getting women back into their "traditional place." This is code for subservient.

A "traditional family" is another code for an undemocratic, authoritarian, male-headed family, and a very punitive family in which children learn early on that it is very dangerous to question authority, no matter how brutal or unjust. That's foundational to the domination model. We cannot dismantle the top of the domination pyramid and still leave its foundations of domination and violence in the primary human relations between women and men and between parents and children largely in place.

So it's not only the status of women. For example, a very important leverage point is changing traditions of violence and abuse in family and other intimate relations. Where do people first learn that it's okay or even "moral" to use violence to impose your will on others? It is in these early family relations. That is why I have co-founded The Spiritual Alliance to Stop Intimate Violence (SAIV). This is a start up. We are just getting going and we do need support for it. I invite people to support us. The SAIV international council includes major world leaders: Queen Noor and Prince El Hassan of Jordan, Archbishop Desmond Tutu of South Africa. Harvey Cox, Professor of the Harvard Divinity School, etc. Men, not only women. The website is www.saiv.net.

We're not talking about women now taking over from men. Matriarchy and patriarchy are just two sides of the domination coin, as

I never tire of pointing out in my writing. The real alternative is the partnership society. We need to pay attention to the primary human relations if we are going to have the foundation for a partnership society.

It's not coincidental that there has been the movement toward a more stereotypically feminine leadership and management style we read about in the corporate literature. Along with the entry of women, not only into worker positions, but also into leadership positions, has also come the change in how leadership is conceptualized and defined. These are not unrelated.

RV: You are very clear about the fact that you're not advocating a feminine model over a masculine model or vice versa, that you're really talking about something that integrates values from both sides. Is that correct?

RE: There are some wonderful values that are considered masculine; logic—not that men are more logical than women, but we think that.

RV: It's a masculine, as opposed to male, quality.

RE: Yes. And assertiveness. Those are great qualities whether they are embodied in a man or a woman. However, some other stereotypically masculine traits such as conquest, domination, those are lousy whether they are in woman or a man. But the problem is that they're so entangled with masculine identity.

RV: Are there comparable qualities on the feminine side that are entangled in women's identities?

RE: Absolutely. For example, the idea that women should be passive. That's a lousy quality whether it's in a woman or a man. We humans are equipped to be active, to be co-creators of our lives, of our societies and of our evolution.

That women are supposed to serve, rather than being served, that women are supposed to be followers, rather than leader, these are lousy ideas for both women and men.

RV: Those seem qualitatively different. They sound more like social norms than qualities compared to the kind of aggressive qualities ascribed to the masculine.

RE: Well, I think that the conversation about what is nature and what is nurture is one of those polarized conversations that don't make much sense. If it is true that men are more biologically predisposed to domination, to violence, then it is all the more reason that we had better take a good look at our socialization processes from day one, don't you think? Because what we're doing is reinforcing that possibility a thousand fold in the way that little boys are brought up and are taught what is masculine.

There are very interesting studies—and I have become very interested in this—in the whole issue of brain neurochemistry and how it develops differently in different environments—and very specifically in a partnership or dominator environment. Remember we were talking about creating the conditions that support or inhibit different kinds of traits and behaviors? For example, there is a gene that is associated with violence in men, but there was a Danish study that showed men with that kind of gene—it was a study of violent criminal behavior—the only ones that engaged in that behavior were the ones that in the studies had been abused as children. By abuse, it includes gross neglect.

The Role of Socialization

RV: That's an example of the socialization that you're talking about?

RE: The interaction of genes and experience

is what we need to pay attention to. Since culture is the most powerful shaper of human experience, we need to pay attention to culture.

RV: How would you suggest that we as leaders go about that in our lives?

RE: I have offered in my work some tools.

RV: In ***The Power of Partnership*** and elsewhere?

RE: Yes, but the most basic tools are the analytical tools of the partnership model and the domination model. We as leaders by using these tools can obtain a much more complete and more realistic assessment of what's holding us back from full human and socio-economic development. That's the first thing. The second thing is leaders have the authority of being able to influence others. So it's not only that we learn how to use these tools, we need to understand what are some of the leverage points that we need to address.

I have identified four key leverage points for cultural transformation, each with a cascade of systemic effects. One is childhood relations. The second is gender relations. The third one is an economics going beyond both capitalism and socialism to what I call an economics of caring that no longer devalues caring and care-giving, because how are we going to have caring policies if we devalue caring and care-giving? It's not realistic. The fourth is beliefs, stories and myths.

If leaders take this seriously, then we can build the foundations for a world of partnership: a sustainable, peaceful, and equitable world. If leaders take this seriously, we can have a highly effective and at the same time more equitable and humane economy. We need to change the rules of the game. We need to encourage and support more caring behaviors rather than penalizing them with the rules of the game. It's very clear that dominator rules of the game do not support caring behavior.

RV: Are you aware of anyone using the dominator/partnership model explicitly to look at leadership?

RE: The fact that my article was chosen as the lead article for the enlightened leadership book will tell you that the editors of that book felt that it was a very important analytical tool and a very important way of looking at leadership.

RV: It seems to me that what you're looking at, what you've described, is pervasive. There is virtually nothing in human relations that can't be understood through that lens.

RE: That's the whole point. Our conventional cultural categories – capitalist vs. communist, right vs. left, religious vs. secular, East vs. West, and so on, they are all fragmented. They just look at economics or they just look at religion or they look at location. As I said, they don't even take into account the primary human relations between women and men and parents and children.

> *"We need to change the rules of the game. We need to encourage and support more caring behaviors rather than penalizing them with the rules of the game."*

RV: I asked you at one time whether you were familiar with the work of Ken Wilber. He is certainly familiar with your work. But I asked you about that, because it seems to me that you are taking a somewhat integral approach to this whole set of phenomena. You are looking at culture. You are looking at systems. You are looking at the beliefs, attitudes and behaviors of individuals. That is a central aspect of integral theory, along with the lines of development that we talked about earlier.

RE: I think that both Ken Wilber's integral approach and Don Beck's *Spiral Dynamics* certainly have very much of the same goals as I do. Our approach is different in the sense that I pay much more attention to conditions that will help us move to these higher stages. I do think that there are higher stages that we are capable of. The other thing that is different is that I don't think that they really take into full consideration the importance of the primary human relations: between the female and male halves of humanity and between them and their sons and daughter. They have good models, but they are incomplete.

RV: Okay. Well, is there anything I haven't asked you that you think I should have?

RE: It's been a fine interview. There is one thing I didn't mention. A number of associates and I did a study for the Center for Partnership Studies called "Women, Men and the Global Quality of Life." For anyone who doubts the centrality of gender relations to our social and economic systems and the existence of a hidden system of gendered evaluations, which so profoundly affects quality of life, they should read that study. We compared two bundles of statistics from 89 nations gathered by established international agencies. One was quality of life measures. The other was measures of the status of women. What we found, of course, is a strong correlation between the two. But we also found that in significant respects the status of women can be a better predictor of general quality of life than GDP. The study can be found at the Center for Partnership Studies website which is www.partnershipway.org.

RV: And if anyone should want to contact you, what route would you recommend?

RE: I would suggest that they go to that website or that they email me at center@partnershipway.org . The other website that would be good is the website for The Spiritual Alliance to Stop Intimate Violence at www.saiv.net . I would like to invite people to support that.

RV: How can people get involved with your work?

RE: They can get involved by volunteering to take a role in building SAIV right now. We are looking for somebody who can help us by being a part-time operations officer. We also need somebody who can help with fund raising. People can also help by simply making donations. They are tax deductible. SAIV is a project of the Center for Partnership Studies, which is nonprofit. The best way for becoming involved with my work is either to join in one of our projects—for example right now we are discussing with an award winning filmmaker, a documentary on my work—or simply by using it. The Partnership Way website has a library with a lot of articles. It has a bookstore; it has a speaker's bureau. It has all kinds of resources.

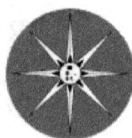

Conscious Leadership

Fred Kofman

RV: Fred, it's great to have a chance to talk with you. What are you up to these days?

FK: I've just finished putting together a financing deal for a new company called Axialent. I will be the President and my partner, Andy Freire, will be the CEO. We're creating an international company that will be working with corporate clients on a world-wide basis and developing an integral perspective on leadership, teamwork and personal effectiveness. I just finished creating the company after almost nine months of negotiations. It really feels like a birth.

RV: Sounds like it might. Is there a story behind the name?

FK: Yes. Axia, means value in Greek. It's about something that is valuable and worthy, not only in terms of ethics but also in terms of economics. "Lent" is the last syllable of excellent. Thus, there is a combination of values and effectiveness or excellence. We merge the drive for effectiveness with consciousness and awareness.

RV: Wonderful. It sounds like this company is the next step on a series of steps you've been taking. I was first aware of your work when you were at MIT, working with Peter Senge. Later you developed your interest in Ken Wilber's work. Tell us a little bit about that journey.

KF: Both Peter Senge and Ken Wilber are on the Advisory Board of Axialent. Peter is going to be our main resource on development of the corporate programs. Ken is our main advisor on the development of personal development programs. So Axialent is the next step on the long evolutionary adventure that has been my life.

I met Peter Senge at MIT in a very circuitous and fortunate way. I was teaching accounting. I saw Peter's book and then connected with him. We really hit it off and started working together. Later, MIT became too constraining for me and I left. I maintained the relationship with Peter; he is one of my best friends and mentors. I started up my company, Leading Learning Communities. That company fulfilled its purpose. It really was a great adventure that enabled me to go to the world and offer some of the things I had put together combining the work of Peter and many others. I find that there is so much wisdom in the field that it is a significant contribution to package, synthesize and develop it in ways that fit the needs of specific clients. I'm hard pressed to claim too much originality. We are all developing this field now in an almost transpersonal way.

I did that work and was quite successful and very happy. At some point I confronted the limits of my own personal ability to manage. I see myself as a teacher more than a CEO or a general manager of the corporation. I don't think I'm terrible at managing, but it is not really my passion. So when Andy Freire showed up, things changed.

Andy told me he had been a CEO in Argentina for many years and was interested in doing something around leadership. He had heard that I had been working with Ken Wilber and he was very excited about that work. We started talking. He had access to financing and we put together this company. We agreed to a division of labor. He is much better than I in managing and I'm much better than he in teaching. So I teach and he manages, and everybody is happy.

RV: What was the nature of the bridge between the work you were doing at MIT with Peter Senge and connection with Ken Wilber?

FK: When I was at MIT I didn't know about Ken. This is a funny story. I kept seeing all of these books by Ken Wilber. I kept thinking that this guy must be like a trashy novelist.
Nobody can write so many books so fast and produce good material, so I was sure that he was the type that must like to rehash the same idea over and over again. Nobody could write so much and be good at it. Once, I was stuck in an airport with nothing to read, so I walked into a bookstore. They had a book by Ken Wilber so I said I guess this is the time when I'm going to read one of his terrible books.

RV: Which one was it?

FK: It was *Eye of the Spirit*, which is not what I would recommend people to start with because it is kind of smack in the middle of his work and assumes a lot of previous knowledge. I just bought it and I started reading it. I remember I had an epiphany, "This guy is really good! I mean, this book is really deep! It is nothing like I thought it was there in the New Age section of the bookstore. I discovered that he was very deep, very profound and I developed a great admiration for him.

RV: What was it about his work that really grabbed you?

FK: I think it was the span and the depth. His

span showed up in all of the areas where he seemed to have something very intelligent to say. This included his analysis of literature, history, spirituality, psychology and anthropology. It was fascinating. Not only his interests were vast, they were also unified. I could see a common theme behind every one of his ideas: the love and freedom of the radiance that appears as what is, as he describes in *Sex, Ecology and Spirituality*. Just inferring the grand model that this man must have had in his head to create these books was very intellectually appealing to me. It also was, for some reason, touching me emotionally. I can't describe why, but there is a beauty in the concepts and the wisdom that I came to see which touched my soul.

> *"Most people who have decision making power are much more developed in their cognitive line, so to speak, than in their emotional, interpersonal or spiritual lines."*

I have done a lot of work with Peter Senge on a practical level. He is masterful. But when I was working with Peter I didn't have an experience of those around Peter and me having a depth of grounding in a very philosophically congruent way. We were working on the surface of profound spiritual and philosophical principles, but those principles were implicit, rather than explicit in our work. When I saw Ken's work I was very taken by it, and I wanted to meet him. But I was deterred by his reputation. I had heard that this guy was like a monk. This was disappointing. For several years I just held my admiration and just read his books while trying to learn as much as possible. I was not sure how to integrate this into the work that I had been doing, so I just kept doing it for the sake of my own personal development.

Then, I decided to move to Colorado. I just wanted sunny weather, to be near the mountains and have a good airport. Colorado is the only place in the Central US that fulfills these requirements. In Boulder I began doing some volunteer work for Naropa University. There I crossed paths with a lady who became Ken's wife. When I saw her she was talking to John Cobb, the President of Naropa University and who was the person I was working with. He called me over and introduced me to her. He asked me for some help with his senior staff at Naropa and I said that I'll do this for you if you introduce me to Ken Wilber. I knew John had a new Ken Wilber manuscript. Anybody to whom Ken would send a manuscript saying, "I would appreciate your comments" had to have a relationship with him. So John sent an email to Ken indicating that I wanted to meet him.

Meeting Ken Wilber

When I met Ken he shocked me. He shattered my image of him because he was incredibly pleasant and warm. I mean, I've read some of the critiques that he has written about other people. The guy has a very sharp pen. I always think: I never want to be on the wrong end of his pen. He was so friendly and warm and he has always been like that. I have known him for a little more than two years and it's been fabulous. It's been a permanent, constant joy and a source of learning. I hesitate to say that he is my friend but I love him dearly and he, for some reason, must find me amusing because he invites me often to visit. And he's agreed to be an advisor to Axialent and to work with us in developing our personal development programs. I feel honored by our relationship.

RV: Clearly his work has influenced yours and you've built on it. Would you sketch out how you see that?

FK: In terms of the business world, one of the problems that I see is that people take a very technical approach to problems. Most people who have decision making power are much more developed in their cognitive line, so to speak, than in their emotional, interpersonal or spiritual lines. Working from the cognitive aspect feels very comfortable for tackling problems that are formalizable. These tend to be scientific approaches that are very powerful to deal with things .

When you have to deal with problems that involve (unconscious) things, the scientific approach is very effective. For many years the tools of total quality management, process reengineering and others that have a scientific or statistical basis really made a huge difference. However, there's a large set of problems that involve, not only the technical aspect -- unconscious things, but also conscious things like human beings. We have the machine but we also have the machine operator. S/he, in addition to performing technical tasks has thoughts, feelings and motivations, fears and concerns, that whole interior world. And the problem usually does not only rest on him or her as an individual but also involves the group of machine operators, with their bosses, the supervisors and their managers and the whole staff of the plant. They form a little community.

A technical approach that focuses on the machine as in a time and motion study is -- as Ken would say -- right in part; but is also wrong in forgetting a significant part of the problem. So I found that Ken's perspective was a very good philosophical model to justify what I had been doing with Peter. There I was focusing on personal mastery and the consciousness of the individual involved, his/her feelings, his/her ability to communicate, to resolve problems by sharing meaning. Not communication in the computer-type sense of hearing the word that I say to convey information to you, but communication where an I and a Thou are creating and sharing meaning. By doing that, we are also providing meaning for our lives. I had been doing that from the early days, but I did not have a philosophical infrastructure to ground it and to argue for it in a sound philosophical way. That solid philosophical foundation is what I found in Ken's integral model.

RV: One of the things that becomes apparent in your work, and it shows up in the set of tapes that you have put out, *Conscious Business*, and also in your article, "Businesssattva: The Business Bodhisattva," is a very strong spiritual dimension in your approach to your work and your life.

FK: I find myself attracted to people and institutions that have a strong commitment to express transcendence into ordinariness. Right now in my work I cover all the bases because I'm Jewish, so that's my own heritage. I work with two Universities: one is is Naropa which is a Buddhist university, and the other is Notre Dame, which is a Catholic university.

RV: With Leo Burke at Notre Dame?

FK: Right. I teach a leadership program in the Integral Executive Program with Leo. My choice is to include all the perspectives.

RV: Get all the bases covered?

FK: Right. You never know. It's portfolio diversification. At the final judgment I can always pull out my C.V. and point to the part that becomes relevant depending on who I find there.

Regardless of the specific tradition there is a common theme that I find in all the spiritual work that attracts me: the unconditional love for the sacredness of what is. . I find myself aligned with people who have roots that go very deep into these spiritual concerns or these transcendent realities—regardless of whether they are Jewish, Catholic, Buddhist, Sufi, or whatever. And who want to extend or bring those roots all the way to a practical current reality.

To say that someone is spiritual is a bit of a misnomer, because we're all spiritual. We are all Spirit. It's like saying, "Your work is very human," or "You're very human." We use human as meaning some form of tenderness, open heartedness or warmth. If you look at the literal meaning of the word, you don't have a choice. You are human. Even if you are a horrible human being, you are still human. There's nothing you can do that would strip you of humanity; you can't lose your official status of human.

In the same sense, I don't believe you can lose your official status of Spirit presencing, because that's what everything is. Some waves are big, some waves are small, but there is no wave that is not water. So the wave is not the thing, but the movement in the medium. That's the way I experience reality.

I believe we exist in a spiritual medium that moves up and down in waves –in fact, we ARE waves ourselves! Our ordinary mind, with its constrained perspective makes us call these waves "things" or "selves": like separate things, like Fred talking to Russ, or there's a mountain called Everest and another mountain, Aconcagua. But it's craziness to see the mountain and deny that it's a folding of the earth. The same earth that rises as Everest, rises also as Aconcagua. Of course, these two Earth-Waves are different, but they are the same Earth. We are all preciously unique individuals, but we're also manifestations of that same precious medium. Paraphrasing Mary Oliver, each one of us is as unique and as common as a field daisy.

"The first question when you are doing anything in life is, "What's the point?" That is a very spiritual question. What are you doing with your one and precious life?"

I don't know if you can call that a spiritual approach. We all have feet, but some of us are aware of our feet and some of us spend our lives looking for them. It makes no difference: clueless or aware, both have the same feet. My work is an attempt not to give feet to people. I don't invite anybody to be spiritual. It's more about just standing on them. Stop looking for your feet and start walking mindfully. Your presence is unconditional. It can manifest in a very powerful and great new way, when you are conscious of what you do. Or you can be living in an aimless drift, as an accident of unconsciousness.

The Spiritual

RV: There has been in recent years more and more literature about the importance of spirit in business, and one of the things about **Conscious Business** that really impressed me was your ability to take these elements of spirit, these elements of a more holistic perspective on work and on business and express them in terms that were really grounded in the experience of people in business. One of the most beautiful examples of that is when you talk about awareness and state that it is the single most important business skill. Please comment on that.

FK: The first question when you are doing anything in life is, "What's the point?" That is a very spiritual question. What are you doing with your one and precious life? You've been given a gift of consciousness and wisdom and now you have this resource for a fairly limited time. What are you going to do with it?

In business you start from the same place. We ask, "What are you doing? What is the point of what you are doing? What are you trying to accomplish? Why is that important to you?" At the same time, to accomplish something in business, unless you want to be a criminal, you have to also value what would further the purpose of other people's lives. That's how you are going to get them to buy your product or service: by giving them something that they find valuable. The source of value is that it is congruent with their life's purpose.

Becoming aware of what is meaningful to you and what is meaningful to those around you is the beginning of every successful enterprise. The moment you lose touch with that you are going to go down in flames. Maybe the words are too spiritual, but this is like basic Business 101. What's your value proposition? Why would anybody want to buy your product or service? You have to think about that in a fairly specific way, because it is not that you think that your product is great. That's not going to make your business successful. Your customers have to think it's great. So you have

to empathize with your customers; you have to become aware not only of what's meaningful to you but what's meaningful to them. To experience them as conscious beings who have a purpose in life and define values that further that purpose in life is really a trans-personal exercise.

It sounds mystical when I say it this way. I don't use this language in companies. I just say, "Let's look at your value proposition and what you think your customers would find valuable in it Do you know your customers? Why do you feel good about offering this to your customers? How does this align with your life and your concerns? How does it align with theirs?"

By engaging in that discussion people develop a passion for what they do. Once the passion is there then you have a question about skillful means. But the technical question, the question of skillful means, (how do you communicate, how do you resolve conflicts, how do you coordinate these actions, how do you do all these things?) becomes relevant only when it's prompted by your passionate commitment to a larger purpose. You don't start teaching people tools without the previous investigation that takes you out of yourself and recontextualizes yourself as serving something that is bigger than just yourself.

Without that recontextualization, technique is really boring. It's like saying, buy a sex manual and sit down to study technique. If there's no love, no technique in the world is going to create an intimate relationship. I think that business is really an act of love. It's different than the intimacy of a couple, but it's a kind of love that supports the opening of other people to find themselves as conscious beings in the world.

RV: Agape rather than Eros?

FK: Well, it's both. It's Eros in the reaching for the ultimate purpose. And it is Agape, bringing down that consciousness, that fire that you have achieved by connecting with that ultimate purpose, and using it to embrace the world and to manifest that energy for freedom in the fullness of manifestation. Those are the two paths that Ken talks about: the ascending path, which tends to be the more masculine desire to be free, to exit the constraints of the world and the more feminine part, which is the descending path into fullness, into the radiance of being. I think the joining of those two parts and the stretching to reach for the fire and for the energy above and embodying that energy in the fullness of the world is really what every fully conscious human being is about

Everybody is "in business." You cannot live without being in business. You may be an employee, a small business owner, a corporate executive, a massage therapist, a nurse, or you may be cleaning houses. Whatever you're doing, part of your being in this world, is being in the domain of work. You have intimacy in the private sphere and work in the public one.

Your intimate transactions are related to sex, and occur in a rather small community, well it depends on what kind of love life you have, but they are usually in a couple or with a small number of partners. But then you have these other transactions, the public ones. They involve the money aspect of your life, giving value to others and receiving value in exchange, as a way to sustain yourself materially, energetically and spiritually.

Sex and money, or intimacy and power, or union and creativity, or communion and agency, are essential aspects of life, as are yin and yang, masculine and feminine, love and freedom. Thanks to Ken, I've met David Deida this year. David is the wisest person I've met in the area of sexuality as a manifestation of spirituality. My conversations with him have made me aware of the beautiful symmetries that exist between sexual value, (sexual attraction, sexiness) and market value (market attractiveness, marketability).

The Role of Leadership in Business

RV: This has bearing on the notion of leadership in business. Do you have a definition of the role of leadership in business?

FK: I'm sure I have many…

RV: Do you have a favorite definition?

FK: Yes. It changes with the situation. I can tell you the one that may feel appealing to me right now, but I don't have one that I would use all the time. Although there's a core and it's always there, the way the core is expressed depends on what I feel the situation is calling for in me. At this moment, I feel like saying that a leader is somebody that can help people align their transcendent individual purposes into a transcendent collective purpose.

"Freedom means that you are so committed to your purpose that you are free even if you die. That nothing is going to make you diverge from your purpose."

RV: What is integral leadership?

FK: Building on the previous definition, an integral leader is one that would do that in, as Ken would say, an AQAL form, meaning in all the quadrants, at all levels of development, engaging all the different lines of personal consciousness, and considering the two tendencies of holons -- agency and communion or the masculine and the feminine, and also involving the multiple of the three states, the gross, the subtle and the causal. So an integral leader is a person that can resonate very powerfully with all the individuals around and has the skill to touch everybody wherever they are and then with that touch awaken in them the passion for creating something that transcends each one of them but involves the community.

RV: Do you have a specific model of leadership that you work from?

FK: I use Ken's model, I use the four quadrants and the idea of the exterior and interior dimensions. The exterior of leadership is behaviors. Also, a leader is like the builder or the architect of the ship in developing the social and business systems of the company. In the interior dimension the leader works in a transformational way, touching people's personality and their interiority. As a cultural icon the leader influences the stories and the shared values and the community.

That is the basic model of leadership that I operate with. However I don't really talk about it too much because I consider that the words are like a hiding place. When people talk a lot about leadership it becomes a subject out there. It becomes a theoretical subject to be discussed as opposed to an experience to be lived. So I focus my work much more in the nitty-gritty practices of leadership, for example, how to be a manifestation of unconditional responsibility, an exemplar of authenticity and integrity.

If you are in the masculine, more agentic mode of Eros, leadership represents the search for freedom or the desire to manifest freedom and power in the world. In this case, being unconditionally responsible is not something you talk about or you give lectures on. It is something you do in your life moment by moment. You are expressing moment by moment that ultimate freedom regardless of the constraints that the circumstances might impose. Freedom doesn't mean lack of constraint. Freedom means that you are so committed to your purpose that you are free even if you die. That nothing is going to make you diverge from your purpose. That's the ultimate freedom. That is the ultimate love. You are leading your life and nobody else has the power to stop you from living your life as it is to be lived. That's an example. That's something that you as a leader do and then other people around just get influenced by it. Your presence is like a strong gravitational field that organizes the Kosmos with "K," as Ken uses it to describe the universe of meanings around you.

If you are in the feminine, more communion mode of Agape, leadership represents the loving blessing of radiance and connection. If you're in the

feminine fullness, your unconditional responsibility is that you're going to hold the consciousness of the unity. You will maintain an openhearted relationship regardless of what the other person does. You are going to be fully in that awareness of connection even when someone is killing you. You are unconditionally present. Nobody can stop you. So that's again a more feminine unconditional response of a leader who can stand there and feel the connection to the other people and to the world and to what's occurring in the situation and she or he would not be swayed.

Love does not mean lack of blocks to relationship. Love means that you are one with your beloved; you ARE the Beloved, always and forever. When you can embody these two notions of unconditional responsibility as unconditional freedom and unconditional love, and make them manifest through your being, that's much more leadership than talking about what does it mean to be a leader. And this is not something you only do in business. You must do it in your whole life.

I don't make such a big deal about leadership because people who don't have formal authority feel excluded: "This isn't about me," they think, "I am not a leader". I think there's a role for the distinction of leadership as the exercise of formal authority, though. It involves leadership consultants, helping executives, people who have authority, to use that authority wisely. I respect and value that. I read their books and learn from them. But for me, leadership is a personal commitment to life. People with formal authority need to do that, but so does anybody who wants to be fully human.

Leadership in Systems

RV: As I listened to you talk about leadership I was equating leadership with formal position authority. For me, in increasingly complex systems the notion of leadership can't be tied to a single role anymore. Leadership is a phenomenon that is shared more widely in the system, so when we're talking about leadership we're talking about both individuals and a system.

FK: I agree with you that thinking of leaders as only people with authority is dangerous, shortsighted and disempowering. That's why I don't like to talk too much about leadership. That word has been hijacked so to speak by the traditional notion that has appropriated the meaning of the word, and I don't share it.

RV: Like heroic leadership?

FK: Yes, exactly -- heroic leadership, functional power or position power, things like that. Now when you start thinking about leadership with other connotations or with other meanings, you have to tell people I am talking about a different kind of leadership, a distinction between heroic leadership and more integral leadership. There is an attraction in that. Now talking about a system, I'm not sure what that means because for me leadership is inherently a human or an attribute of consciousness, a conscious empathy. And I don't see a system as the subject with localized consciousness.

RV: Let me see if I can offer a way of looking at that and get your response. What I was trying to suggest earlier is that with increasingly complex organizational systems, business systems, whether we're talking just in terms of size or geography or other measures of complexity, that it's increasingly difficult for one person to exercise leadership, that it is something that is shared, that there are leaders throughout the system.

FK: Oh, yes, absolutely.

RV: If that's the case and we think about the phenomenon of leadership within a business system, within a business organization, then there is some kind of system of leadership, that there's some kind of relationship among those that are performing leadership roles that could be characterized as having a culture and a system.

FK: Okay, I understand now. That makes a lot more

sense. It's not that the system is leader, but this sense of interrelationships amongst the leaders that you call a system of leadership. That makes a lot more sense. In fact, I will agree with you 100% that as the level of complexity grows, it's impossible for any one person to hold that complexity and to manage it. In fact, that's why Leading Learning Communities, my old company, where I was a single leader, lost its appeal to me, and Axialent, where I share the leadership with Andy and all our general managers and principal consultants, became my new enterprise.

I do think that there's a role for a person to be a leader of a system. He or she won't be able to micro-lead everything. He or she will have to take a much broader approach, and say, "Okay, on these large strategic lines we're going to have an alignment and we're going to have a common vision, a purpose and a way of operating together." But then there will be a hierarchical system or a holarchical system to use more of Ken's lexicon.

> *"...as the level of complexity grows, it's impossible for any one person to hold that complexity and to manage it."*

In this system there would be a higher level of perspective of the whole. The different parts of the subsystem will also have lower levels of leadership that are managing their own sub-system at the same time coordinating the functioning of that subsystem with the other subsystems that compose the system. So I think the areas of communication, conflict resolution and coordination of functions that I focus on, are very, very important because that's where the rubber meets the road. That's where people are able to come together and create something that's bigger than any one of them.

Hierarchies

RV: You wrote an article in relation to Wilber's thinking, "Holons, Heaps and Artifacts, and Their Corresponding Hierarchies." Has that been published anywhere?

FK: No. We just published it on the web at the World of Ken Wilber site. That created quite a bit of a stir. I feel bad because a lot of people sent me their comments and I wasn't able to reply. I really wrote the paper summarizing my conversations with Ken as a kind of a service to the community.

I went to see Ken and I said, "Ken, what about this?" He said, "Yeah, you're right. There's something here that needs to be developed further." Then people spent a lot of time and attention on the article. I think they came up with some wonderful ideas. It's just that I'm not a philosopher and I have a business to run. I feel bad I didn't respond, but I think I would have felt worse had I taken the time to respond and postponed my other priorities.

RV: If you're willing I'd like to talk about some of these ideas and reflect on an approach to leadership that I've tried to articulate in the *Integral Leadership Review* and elsewhere. It might be helpful if we start by differentiating a social and an individual holon. That's spelled out in the article and if I could have your permission I would like to place this article on my website (www.leadcoach.com) in the resource section.

FK: Oh, absolutely.

RV: I'm not going to ask you to summarize what is in it, because people can go to the article and read that. One of the statements you make is that "dehumanizing consequences ensue from combining individual and social holons in the same holarchy." You give as an example the relationship between an individual and a team, and you offer several organizational examples. I'd like to run this other model by you for you to consider through your lens.

It begins with the idea that we were just talking about, that leadership is something that's shared in complex systems. And at least a place to begin to look at this is with executive leadership in an organization, at least beginning with the executive leadership in a system. In the article, you offer examples. One is Sergeant Pepper's Lonely Hearts Club Band (an album and song by The Beatles). I want to talk about that in relationship to the model that I was telling you about and referring to earlier.

My image is that what would happen in any kind of generic situation is that you would have a group of people coming together around some shared purpose, whatever that purpose may be. In my early work in this we were often using the idea of the Elvis Presley Fan Club. They would get together and say we want to perpetuate the music of Elvis, and they'd come together around that.

The next step would be that they would have to find some way of putting together resources and describing roles and relationships, processes and structures to support them in doing that. They would form a leadership organization, if you will.

Then they would find that there are things going on that are at the level of complexity that they couldn't handle with formal organizational operations and they'd have to develop the capacity for team work. From that place of having developed some level of capacity for team work they would be able to engage more effectively with the stakeholders of the club, of the group that was originally formed.

The model suggests that at each level of development (and certainly these could be refined in more detail) there is a concomitant role for the individual leader. For example, there's membership in a group, a contributor to an organization, a player on a team, and so forth. If we can conceptualize leadership in a complex system with this kind of lens, including the internal and the external aspects of that, at the individual level we've got a framework that we can use to look at the phenomenon of leadership. We would recognize that development in each of these quadrants has all of the attributes that you've spelled out in the article and that is reflected in the work of *Spiral Dynamics*®, the AQAL (All Quadrants, All Levels) literature and the work that Ken has been doing with Don Beck, and so forth.

The thing I'm confused about or not clear about is by spelling it out that way am I simply mixing up individual and social holons? Am I throwing in artifacts? Or is this a useful way of at least representing an archetype, a developmental archetype of leadership in a complex system?

FK: I don't find any problem with this. Nothing of what you said irritates my sensibility. Let me tell you what would irritate me and what I was thinking when I wrote the article.

This is my main concern. As long as you say membership you are distinguishing an individual holon from the social holon. You're not conflating those two hierarchies. The problem is when you say the individual is a part of the team. This is not the same thing as saying the individual is a member of the team. That's what this discussion is all about.

To be very graphic I'll use political examples. In a political situation you can have a system like the one that the founding fathers were trying to implement with the Constitution of the United States that says all men are created equal. They are inalienably free. They own themselves and their lives. Now individuals who are self-owners can choose to associate and create an organization of which they are members. When people affiliate they can create social entities in which they participate as members. But they are not a part of that organization.

On the other arm, I mean, hand, my arm is a part of my body. My arm is not a member of my body. There are no members because the arm doesn't have any individual agency. My arm doesn't operate by itself. It's not an entity with conscious volition. So the arm is a part of me and I, as an individual, have a different kind of control over my arm than the government can have on me.

But the moment you mix those two things you get into Mao killing 50 million people or Stalin saying it's okay to kill 30 million people, because they are like a gangrenous arm in the "social body". These people are a bad part of society and we need to cut off this part, because they're hurting the body. It

would be like you cutting off your arm if you had gangrene. You wouldn't say that it was murder or a crime but that you — as owner of yourself — realized that a part of your body was harming you so you cut it off. But the moment you translate that to a social holon and say the family or the clan is the primary thing, the people are part of the clan and if you don't conform to the clan we're going to cut you off just like you would cut off a gangrened arm, that's when it gets very dangerous.

RV: You use the example again with the Sergeant Pepper's Friendly Heart Club Band of one of the participants in the Band who is developmentally challenged in some way. While all the other members go to orange, the person who is developmentally challenged is stuck in blue. The person stuck in blue is not truly a part of the larger team effort, because the others are operating at a higher level of consciousness and capacity than the person at blue. Have I interpreted that correctly?

FK: Several people challenged me on that, but that's not at all what I wanted to say. For example, in my family we're all members of the family, my wife and I and we have six children. The youngest is three; the oldest is 13. We're all members of the family and we're all equal members. Nobody is more a member than anybody else. We are all full members of the family. Nobody is part of the family because each one of us is an individual. The family is a social holon, so it does not have parts; the family has members, who are individuals affiliated in a system of social interaction and shared meaning. Are we together so far?

RV: Absolutely.

FK: We are all equal members. However, when you look for the level of evolution of this family, at what level of consciousness this family operates when we're all together, if you're looking for the lowest common denominator it is my three year old daughter, Michelle. She is the one who is at the lowest stage of development. She's only three. The common language we share as a family is the language of the three year old. If we all want to go to the movies together, we choose a movie that she can understand, that she can enjoy. We watch the movie, and we all enjoy it, too. It is probably not the movie we would go to see if she wasn't there.

My next daughter, Paloma, is eight. If my three-year-old daughter weren't there, we would probably choose a movie that an eight year old would understand and enjoy. Now that doesn't mean that my three year old is not a full member of the family. It just means that she participates in a social holon that operates at the level of development of a three year old, because she cannot participate at a higher level.

I have a ten-year old son who loves math. He always asks me "Dad, can you give me math problems?" When I'm talking with my son, Tomás, about math problems and we do a simple algebraic operation, my three year old is not a member of that system. She cannot be a participant of that social interaction, because it's beyond her grasp. That doesn't mean she's not a full member of the family. It just means that my math conversation with Tomás is totally going over her head and she can only participate in the lower band of conversations that reach up to a three year old. Above that, she cannot be a participant, although in all other aspects she is still a full member of the family.

> *"...when you have a leader who has a high level of development, if that leader pretends to engage everybody at his or her level, she is going to lose the affiliation of a large part of the organization that perhaps is not able to function there."*

The same thing with my wife: my wife and I are a subset of the family but we have a level of development and a kind of conversation that we engage and we affiliate around that is ungraspable by our children. Now that doesn't mean our children are any less important or less loved or less members of the family. It just means they can operate as fully functioning members up to a certain level of consciousness according to their personal evolution. Am I making sense?

RV: Yes.

FK: Now let me go back to the Band. It is an organization and there you have a person who has achieved a certain stage of development below what other people have. This doesn't mean that this person is any less a member of the organization. It's not a handicap, even if he were a completely retarded person. That doesn't mean he cannot be loved and included and participate, just like if I have another baby, well our baby will still be a member of the family even though she couldn't even go to the movies. We truly include every person in our heart and our love, but that doesn't mean that we all are going to disregard that our baby, or our three year old, is at a lower level of development and she cannot participate in some conversations.

In a company or in a group some members may not be able to affiliate around a higher stage of development because it goes over their heads, given where they are in their lives right now. What I meant is that when you have a leader who has a high level of development, if that leader pretends to engage everybody at his or her level, she is going to lose the affiliation of a large part of the organization that perhaps is not able to function there. It would be like me trying to get my three year old to discuss Ken Wilber's model with me and, if she cannot discuss it, I said, "You're useless! Why do I want you in my family?" That would be so unkind, it would be horrible!

In a company, or a community–a social holon–compassion means understanding that not everybody is operating at your level, that some people cannot yet attain the depth of consciousness that you have the gift to hold at this point in your life. The compassionate thing to do is to relate to them in the most developmental way that you can think of or that you can feel in your heart, but not to push them into an area where there is no common denominator.

The Unity of the Holon

RV: This raises a question that I also try and address and you've talked about. That is alignment or attunement. In the holon essentially what we've got are four boxes, four categories. I'm less clear about how Ken or you talk about the relationships among the quadrants. So for example, in the model that I've put together around integral leadership, I've talked about the relationship between the interior individual and the interior collective as one of alignment, or nonalignment as the case may be. There is also a dynamic aligning process continually at work there in the relationship between the internal individual and external individual, beliefs and behaviors. In that relationship there is a self-management process that goes on. In the relationship between individual and collective behavior there is an engagement process. In order for the system to evolve over time all of those other processes must be going on.

In your understanding of the integral approach is there a more effective way of thinking about development that links the quadrants rather than just what is interior to the quadrants?

FK: This has been one of the most obscure areas in Ken's work. It's not obscure because he hasn't explained it well. It's obscure because it's just a very tricky notion to grasp. Let me give you a metaphor. Think of an object in three dimensions. Think of anything you can hold, like a telephone you're holding in your hand. Each object has height, width and depth. You can map the object in three-dimensional space and you can calculate these three dimensions. There is not necessarily a connection between height and width. Some objects are very long and very thin and some objects are short and thick, etc.

When you're talking about the holon, you're not really talking about four things or boxes that need to be connected; you're talking about one thing that is expressed and is manifest in four dimensions, just like the telephone, manifests in three dimensions.

It's one thing that, depending on what axis you use to look at it, it's going to display a certain face. Does that make sense so far?

RV: Having a leadership group would be the whole but those other elements would be the parts of that whole. Is that not accurate?

FK: Let me talk first about the individual. That may be a little easier place to start. An individual has an interiority of certain thoughts and feelings. You can understand an individual or you can see an individual as a space of consciousness. The individual also has a body, a certain weight and physical characteristics, neurological connections in the brain, a skeleton and we can calculate weight and height and all those things.

"As a conscious being, I have a fourfold nature. I am individual and I am collective. I am interior and I am exterior."

RV: The biology, essentially?

FK: Yes, the biological constitution.

As to the individual you are looking at two dimensions. One could be the thoughts and feelings; the other could be the bodily structure. Now of course you could then ask what is the connection? What is the relationship between these two dimensions, because they're not completely independent? If your brain goes haywire because we put some drugs in it, that's going to affect your interior experience. Or if you have certain thoughts, that could trigger reactions in the physical structure. If you get scared there would be hormones, like adrenaline and cortizon, which would be released into your bloodstream. Or vice versa. You can be injected with some hormones and then have the experience of fear. There is a link between them like one branch of the tree into another branch. It's the same tree; it's just that you're looking at it from two different perspectives.

Just like that you can see that any individual exists in a space of relationships. So it's not that two individuals need to get together to have a social holon. Every holon, by the great fact of being conscious exists in a relational space. So for me, as an individual, it's not just that I have interiority as a person. I also exist in a space of shared meanings with my community and those have always been there for me. I was born into that space just like I'm born into a reality that transcends me. I breathe and I get breast fed by my mother and all that, but I cannot survive physically by myself. I survive in a permanent interaction with the space around me as an open system. By the same token, my interiority is born in an already meaningful space. The self is always already swimming in a linguistic soup, a soup cooked by a community.

As a conscious being, I have a fourfold nature. I am individual and I am collective. I am interior and I am exterior. It's almost like an address. You have the street and the number. When you look at a holon you can locate that holon as a point in this four-dimensional space, as a four dimensional vector, but it's only one entity. It's not four entities. And that's the problem of talking about a social holons as a group of people getting together. The social aspect of the holon is always already in a network of physical relationships, like I'm a member of a society and there are social rituals and practices for life, and I always exist in a network of meanings that my community shares.

RV: I'm trying to understand the implications of that. It seems to me that what you're saying is the holon is describing what is, but is not necessarily describing by itself any kind of change or developmental patterns. That you've got to move to the holarchy (a hierarchy of holons) to do that.

FK: Exactly, but moving up the holarchy does not mean going from a person to a group. There are higher and higher levels of development of the person.

RV: Is there a higher level holon than the person?

FK: No. A human being is the ultimate holon. The human being can hold within one body, our exterior structure, the whole evolution of consciousness up to the divine cosmic realization. There's nothing further that is necessary than an individual human being. The individual is at the top of a holarchy that goes all the way down to atoms. As Ken likes to say, from dust to Divinity.

It's actually very intricate. When I read *Sex, Ecology and Spirituality* I think I understand it and find the whole holarchy deal a very appealing story. But then, I am never really sure that I really, really understand it. It took me many hours of conversation with Ken before I realized that my first, naive reading of his books had left unanswered many questions, left unfilled many conceptual holes. Ken's is a very delicate and very profound philosophical system, almost impossibly intricate.

Every now and then, I go back to him and say, "Ken, tell me again what the hell are you talking about?" He is very patient and explains it to me again. And then I think, "Okay, now I get it." Then 2-3 days later I can't believe I was so crazy as to believe I got it. I know what he told me but it doesn't make sense anymore. One of the mistakes that most people make about Ken's work is to over simplify the notion of the holon, to say, "Oh well. You have a holarchy and it's like having a radio and the radio is part of a stereo, which is part of a sound system, which is part of…."

"I don't think Picasso painted because he was afraid that he wouldn't have enough money to pay the rent. I don't think Bill Gates is too worried about supporting himself in his old age."

RV: Those are artifacts.

FK: Exactly. Those are artifacts. Those are unconscious things, created by a conscious thing, but unconscious in themselves. And if you say you have the person and the person is part of the team and the team is part of the organization, it's a huge mistake. The person is not part of the team. The person is not part of anything. An individual human being is the highest holon.

Development

RV: In the model I was presenting I think of it more as roles than I think about it as the person. It's the person when they're in that role but it's not the whole person. I wonder if maybe we could shift just a little bit, because you talked about your work with Leo Burke, and it raises a very challenging question for us and that's the notion of development. What we've just been talking about has some implications for development. The whole area of spirit that you've talked about does, as well.

I think of development as fulfilling the potential that each of us has. There's some evidence or suggestion from [Clare] Graves (source of Spiral Dynamics) and others' work that the number of levels of development that any individual can expect to be able to transcend in a lifetime is limited. I'm wondering if you, especially with your deep connection to spirit, could reflect on where you see the potential for development for business leaders or any of us?

FK: It's not very fruitful to confuse spirit and development. There are notions out there that if you work hard enough and you grow enough you will reach the ultimate level of development, which is Spirit. That is not entirely wrong, but it is not entirely right either.

Ken has a long discussion in *Integral Psychology*, about what is called spiritual. He distinguishes two notions: a spiritual line of development, which is concerned with the source of ultimate meaning, and a spiritual level of any line, which is the highest level of any such line—for example, a spiritual cognitive level. So if you refer to this latter concept, it is Ok to say that Spirit is "at the end of the rainbow," so to speak.

But I find that a bit misleading because it can take

you to believe that you will become "spiritual" only when you achieve the highest reaches of the human potential in all endeavors. A feast for the super-ego! Now you're screwed, because you will NEVER get there. (And your inner critic will remind you often of your shortcomings as a human/spiritual being.)

Let me use me and my running as an example. Given my biology, my history and my current lifestyle, there is only so much speed that I can develop in my life. If I like to run, I'm not going to run a mile in less than four minutes. There is just no way I could do that with my body and my age and my training. Maybe if I had started when I was a child I could have made it but now, "no way, Jose."

I can't play basketball like Michael Jordan. No matter how much I practice, I just don't have what it takes to do it. You may say that's too bad. I'll never be a fully realized individual because I cannot grow to run fast or play basketball like Michael Jordan. But if you think that in order to fully realize myself as a human being I have to do those things, you're nuts.

What's a poor human being to do, given that we'll never reach perfection? For me, the answer is that you have to call off the search. You have to stop torturing yourself, thinking that spiritual experience only occurs at the highest level of development; that you have to go to stratospheric heights in consciousness in order to experience your full divine nature. That is just not true. That is a nightmare where the present gets alienated to never-arriving future.

If you just relax and take a breath, wherever you are right now, in your current level of development, if you just let go of the striving, consciousness will shine from you, through you, as you, out into everything, and will look back at you from everything, through everything, as everything. That's all it is and there's nothing more. You can be an alcoholic and maybe you cannot get out of your addiction. Or maybe you are in emotional pain and you do not know what to do. That doesn't make you any less human. Therefore that doesn't make you any less divine.

I just remember a phrase I read somewhere, I wish I could recall where: "You are not a human being having a spiritual experience; you are a spiritual being, having a human experience."

So perhaps the notions of spirituality and development are best kept separate. Development goes really slow and is quite unusual beyond a certain level. Most of us will be stuck in a certain range. Some of us may get farther along some line than others, but as human beings we are fairly limited in our capacity to achieve the highest level of our potential, the highest rung of the ladder going from the unconscious to the Super-conscious.

The good news is that Spirit is not the upper rung of the ladder, but the wood out of which the ladder is made. In addition to climbing the ladder (please don't get me wrong, I LOVE development!), we need to get in touch with its essence. Essential depth relieves you from the stress of never-quite-being-there. You don't have to get to the upper rung to be in touch with the wood. Wherever you are, right there, you are touching it with your very hands.

It's ridiculous to say there's more spirit inside the church than outside the church, or there's more spirit in Jerusalem than in New York. Spirit and God is ever-present in any of its manifestations. Plato said the universe is the visible side of God. That means trashy music is the visible side of God as much as a sublime Symphony. At that level there is no difference.

RV: I see and hear expressed many kinds of aspirations around developmental models like Spiral Dynamics®. Would you say that's misplaced?

FK: It depends. There are two drivers. One is fear and the other is love. When you are driven by fear then it's completely misplaced. The fear driver is exemplified by the thought, "Unless I get to

Turquoise or Coral, I'm nothing. I'm not evolved and I will not be saved. If I want to 'get to heaven', I need to develop to the higher stages of the spiral." That's just like the person who claims unless I make it to vice president, I'm worthless or unless I have $5 million in the bank, I'm ashamed of myself or unless I have a beautiful wife or a successful husband then I have no self esteem.

The fear is that you are and will remain empty unless you get something to fill you up. The sad truth is that if you think you're empty, you're like a black hole: nothing is going to fill you up. No matter what object you try to use to assuage your fear, it's never going to work. Some people are trying to get a lot of money. Some people are trying to get a lot of enlightenment. Whether material or spiritual, it's all the same materialism. You're still trying to get something that will fill up the emptiness that you believe you are. Saying that to be realized I need to evolve to a higher state is like saying that I need to have a Mercedes Benz, a lot of money, great clothes, or to be successful in order to be worthy.

At some point in your life you might change. You might realize "Wait a minute! I'm not empty. I'm full. I am more than full. I am overflowing with fullness and freedom." Then, you leave fear and you enter love. Now your life becomes a quest to express that fullness and that freedom. Now you are not looking to fill yourself up by achieving something. You are actually looking for ways in which you can express the fullness and freedom that you already are. You don't work to make money, although money is part of the deal; you work to express your creative potential in the service of others. That's when you do your best work.

I don't think Picasso painted because he was afraid that he wouldn't have enough money to pay the rent. I don't think Bill Gates is too worried about supporting himself in his old age. There can be other drivers, such as power or prestige. I don't know much about Bill Gates or Picasso as individuals, I'm just using their cases as a metaphor to illustrate this potential to work beyond the fear-incentive provided by material needs.

When you operate from love you can say that as a human being you want to be the fullest possible expression of consciousness. And you want to be in this world to invite other people to wake up to who they truly are, not because unless you do that you are nothing, but because you cannot stop it. It's almost an irrepressible urge. It's like breathing. Once you inspire and you taste air, you cannot hold your breath.

When I feel myself so full I'm just bursting with energy and creative potential, I'm going to do something with it. Then I'm acting out of love. Now out of love I do many things. I can work on myself. I can try to refine my skills at running, basketball, piano, business, teaching or at anything; I can even try to advance up the spiral dynamics stages of consciousness. But I'm not doing that because I'm afraid that if I don't succeed I'm worthless. I'm doing that because it seems like a skillful way to express my freedom and my fullness, my worth-- which is ultimately not mine but Spirit's. It is just expressing the ultimate richness of Spirit in this plane. I am a conscious vehicle for that expression, which is the greatest joy that exists.

That's why I tell you it's not wrong to try to develop. I would not discourage anybody from trying to grow. The question is, why are you trying to grow? And if you think that unless you grow you are worthless, you are operating out of fear and you will never get out of the nightmare. Once you are at peace with yourself and you find the truth of who you are essentially, your quest for growth becomes simply the quest to express the most beautiful and radiant way the truth of existence.

RV: That's a beautiful lesson, Fred. Earlier in the interview you mentioned how much you like to teach. And clearly, from the things you have been sharing with us you have a lot to share. Are you still teaching and how can people access that?

FK: If anybody's interested they can send me an email from the web sites: www.leadlearn.com or www.axialent.com.

RV: Thank you. Do you have any book length publications in the works?

FK: I wrote a trilogy in Spanish called Metamanagement that I'm translating right now. I believe that before the end of the year it will be published. [Published as *Conscious Business*]

RV: Wonderful. I hope you will let me know when it's available.

FK: Yes, I'll be happy to.

RV: Thank you so very much.

FK: You're very welcome.

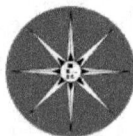

Leaders and Developoment

Susanne Cook-Greuter

RV: Your work has been very much based on the research of Loevinger and you've expanded her model. Would you talk just a little bit about that expansion?

SCG: When I discovered Loevinger's instrument I was so excited, because it combined my interest in language with psychological theory about adult development. By looking at how people express themselves you can predict to some degree what kind of worldview they are most likely using. After I learned how to score the Loevinger instrument in 1979, very soon I got protocols that were from the high end, second tier of development. Loevinger's theory and her measurement just weren't clear enough. It didn't differentiate between the stages in the sense that I felt one could.

I initially just said, "Well let's see what I can find." I just started collecting data, more and more data. You can have intuitions about things, but unless you have empirical data, a lot of data, it's not yet science.

RV: Then it seemed there were people who were falling outside the boundaries on the high end of her scale?

SCG: Yes. Or simply that the distinctions she made weren't enough. I felt that there could be finer distinctions that really would be important to describe that territory. Her model stops at the integrated stage as a sort of catchall for self-actualizers and above. I felt compelled to search because there has been a personal intrigue about the

higher end for me.

RV: And the category that you came up with beyond Loevinger's model?

SCG: It is one that focuses on becoming aware of one's own meaning making. It is above yellow (Spiral Dynamics®), above Kegan's stage five where I felt there needed to be more clear distinctions. I started in 1979 to collect data. By 1985 I had a vague theory. I had been discouraged certainly by Loevinger, herself, to even try that kind of approach. She simply said you can't do it—nobody can—and if you believe you can you must be suffering from hubris.

[laughter]

All of us exploring the mature end of development have to ask those questions of ourselves: Is that really what I am doing here? Am I really falling into that category? Am I taking on things that I am not qualified to look at? Who determines that? Her injunction caused quite a quandry for me for a while.

RV: What are the stages that you have focused on?

SCG: Beyond the Autonomous stage is my focus. The ideal of this stage would be somebody who really knows himself very well, knows the patterns of development and meaning making of other people; a person who is tolerant; a person who could look at multiple systems and compare them, somebody who is very accomplished in some ways compared to most of society.

For the Autonomous stage, we're talking here about maybe 6-8% of the population. They tend to be consultants or people who are interested in that sort of relationship to others. They are interested in helping others grow. That is really one of their chief characteristics. After reading thousands of protocols, Autonomous individuals, or Strategists to use [Bill] Torbert's term, also give the impression of ego attachment in the sense of wanting to present a really coherent, caring and complex self. It's all driven from the ego; it's all driven from "Look how well I do these things." Unlike earlier stages, they don't hide conflict necessarily any more, they may show the shadow sides of themselves.

> *"There are theories that offer a whole spectrum of development of the self from birth to mature adulthood and there are theories that focus merely on cognitive capacity in manipulating abstract symbols."*

RV: So subsequent stages are about ego detachment?

SCG: Yes. More and more so. Ego-deconstruction starts with the post-conventional stages. During conventional development from birth to stage four or the Achiever stage, the independent, separate self gets constructed. Stage four is the western ideal of what an adult should be: an independent, self-governing agent who makes rational decisions. That is still what we are trying to get the people to become through our education systems. However, the experience of separateness also constitutes a major illusion in that we are totally interdependent with other people and the environment.

Then somebody who knows who they are starts to question the self-identity with clear boundaries that they have constructed. It is with the Individualist stage that questioning of assumption starts: Who said so; why do I think the way I think about this? The questioning starts the deconstruction of what

one believes. The doors of perception open and disillusionment takes place. The first step is just to sort of become aware of the culturally embedded stuff. The second step of deconstruction was what my research was about. It involves becoming aware of the fundamental way we make meaning in our own lives and how our constructions really profoundly affect how we experience life.

Language Awareness

RV: This is where the awareness of language comes in?

SCG: Yes. I think language awareness is a major distinguisher among different theories. There are theories that offer a whole spectrum of development of the self from birth to mature adulthood and there are theories that focus merely on cognitive capacity in manipulating abstract symbols. The latter often do not acknowledge the limits of symbolic representation that they themselves are bound by. If a theory doesn't acknowledge that, it is limited to the personal rational realm and does not represent an understanding of human meaning making.

RV: What's the next stage?

SCG: Ahh, the next stage! This theoretical dilemma always makes me laugh. All researchers get to an area where it's their own cognitive or developmental edge. Whatever comes after that gets put into their highest finally hypothesized stage. I critiqued Loevinger's last stage, the Integrated, for just being sort of a collection of various ill-defined things. The irony is that this is the case for my last stage as well.

Researchers can push a little bit beyond the limit of their own capacity. But then the last stage in a theory is usually a projection of what one intuits about that stage or what one would like to be at oneself.

RV: When we're in a stage ourselves and we're looking upward, we're going to define anything up there in terms of the stage we're in, is that correct?

SCG: That's one way of looking at it. Even if we have really good intuitions, we can't necessarily measure them. Using a sentence completion test totally limits one from assessing anything beyond language. There would have to be a different approach and instrument in order to make differentiation beyond the personal level.

RV: That suggests a question that one of the readers of the *Integral Leadership Review* raised. Have there been any studies that you're aware of that compare results from your approach, the Leadership Development Profile, with Kegan's and others' instruments that have been developed to look at stage development of individuals?

SCG: Not much. Only from my own study of the measures. You know Kegan was one of my teachers, so I had a good experience, good thorough knowledge of his approach. Most current adult development theories tend to stop around the second tier and are limited to the personal, rational domain.

RV: I don't mean just in terms of the stage model, but in the use of the assessments, how people come out on the different assessments.

SCG: Depending on how the assessment is done it comes out differently. Spiral Dynamics® uses a multiple-choice test that is fairly transparent. The values test is just too simple. People who have read enough and think of themselves as yellow can come out yellow or higher. Given that we know which responses would be desirable, we can choose those at the level of espoused values. I've found that test to be the least appealing aspect of the whole wonderful Spiral Dynamics® system.

Robert Kegan

RV: Isn't there an approach used for Kegan's stages as well?

SCG: Yes, and that one is beautiful in another way. It gives rich qualitative data. It's an interview measure.

RV: It's the Subject/Object Interview?

SCG: Yes. It is very time consuming. One of the issues that I'm concerned about there is that the developmental level of the interviewer could cause bias in what he or she controls. If the interviewer is less developed than the interviewee, you know they cannot bring out easily what is beyond their own purview, their own field of vision. Things simply cannot appear on their radar. That we cannot understand or even register distinctions several levels above our own is a basic tenet of developmental theory.

RV: Have you done any comparisons between LDP results and Subject/Object Interview results?

SCG: We have only individual cases where that was done. With a good interviewer and because the S/O interview is probed, it might come out a little higher than it would on the LDP. The LDP is not probed. People really project their own view of what they're doing on the test.

One can always say in a projected test, if the person chooses whatever they choose to do with the test, this is part of their behavior. In that sense, it reflects something that's probably real about them.

RV: That's the part I don't want to own.

[Laughter]

What was going on for me when I did it was that I have a bias towards these kinds of tests and my bias is that they're never going to tell you the truth about you. They're only going to tell you about how your responses correspond to somebody's model. I tend to take tests rather quickly. I did that with LDP and, as a consequence, my answers tended to be rather brief. I didn't really respond to the questions as fully as I might have.

SCG: But it's an interesting choice you made that does reflect your stated bias.

RV: Yes, it is.

SCG: And that's the point that I would then say is worth looking at. Where is that sort of bias or preference coming from? See, whatever one does with a projective test, does seem to show something about one's way of life.

RV: Yes, well it sure did that.

SCG: And I would always also say for any of these measures, when they're being taken by people who are specialists in the field, that in itself is an absolutely confounding factor. If you know too much about any measure there is the likelihood that it's not a good representation of you, whatever comes out.

Jane Loevinger

RV: Did Loevinger ever have an opportunity to see any of the results of the research that you were doing?

SCG: She had opportunities, but she…it's almost a funny story. Perhaps I can tell it. Shortly after I sent her my dissertation proposal we celebrated her 80th birthday in 1998. They organized a conference in her honor and I attended. I asked her, "Did you get a chance to look at my proposal?" She just sort of glanced at me and said, "Yeah, I took it with me when I had to go to the dentist for some root canal work." I just thought this was so symptomatic for our relationship.

[Laughter]

She just really had doubts about anybody being able to say anything beyond her model. Another indicator is that in the new manual that came out in 1996—Hy and Loevinger worked 10 years on that new manual—they actually gave many

fewer examples for their highest stage than they had in the original version. They said that for all practical purposes the integrated stage could not be measured.

RV: You feel you've come up with a method and criteria to measure beyond the Autonomous stage and you've demonstrated this in your dissertation, ***Postautonomous Ego Development: Its Nature and Measurement***, that was published in 1999.

SCG: That was really the whole intent. Many people have theories, but do they have the empirical evidence to actually test whether their conjectures make sense? To check whether others come up with the same interpretation as yours is part of what validity testing is about. Does your interpretation of the data make sense to others or does it just reflect your own idiosyncratic view?

"I'm always one of the few that insists that we don't overvalue what I call vertical development or transformation by helping people get to higher stages vs. just helping them to become more fully at home where they currently are (horizontal growth)."

RV: At the heart of all of this is the question of adult development and learning. The constructivist developmental approach that you're taking has different points of view on the question of how does one develop across stages, how does one learn and evolve over time. Where do you stand on that?

SCG: In the early stages development seems to be maturational. All children seem to go through pretty much the same stages that almost all developmental theorists call the pre-conventional stages and early conventional stages.

RV: An affirmation of Piaget's work, then?

SCG: Yes, exactly. The adult development field proper really started when Michael Commons and other researchers began to document adult ways of thinking that went beyond what Piaget had postulated. It turned out that Piaget's formal operations, which is reached by early adulthood, is not the most complex way of how adults make meaning. We now believe that development in terms of increasing complexity and integration can continue throughout the lifespan. But there is still some debate about that. Are the higher stages simply more complex forms of formal operations or are they fundamentally different? That's the ongoing debate.

Working in Organizations

RV: Well, it's a critical debate when it comes to questions of how do we bring this knowledge and this perspective to bear on working with people and organizations, particularly for the area of my interest in leadership. I know you're working with Bill Torbert and Harthill. What is your perspective on applying your work to the notion of leadership in business and organizations, communities, etc.?

SCG: I'm always one of the few that insists that we don't overvalue what I call vertical development or transformation by helping people get to higher stages vs. just helping them to become more fully at home where they currently are (horizontal growth). In general, we know from data that for leading organizations or for transformational leadership, postconventional development is an advantage. Only with postconventional development do you have a sense of the whole spiral. I think Spiral Dynamics® makes the point very well that unless you can do that, unless you recognize the value and contribution as well as the limits of each prior level, you can't really tailor your leadership approach to others. You can't really appreciate what others bring to the table and how necessary all perspectives are to a viable organization.

Talking SD language, if you are orange, you will only see what's wrong with blue. It is very hard for any of the conventional stages to see what the others have to offer. Only at yellow or at the Autonomous or Strategist's stage do you have that

inclusive awareness in the sense of an awareness of your own development or evolution as a part of how the world works and therefore an appreciation of where others are on the trajectory.

RV: Do you think that can be taught?

SCG: I think supportive environments and mentoring can help people get there, but you can't force it. No amount of training will get somebody there who has no inner readiness for it, or the cognitive capacity to go further. Here I get into an interesting dilemma for myself because my spiritual path has certain esoteric explanations of why this is so. And yet I don't want to use that kind of explanation when I'm doing theory with empirical data. I want to see from the data itself just what kinds of explanation come forth. It does make sense to me that not all people are predestined to reach the later stages.

RV: Reaching a higher stage or not, what about those who are still first tier and looking down? Can we develop oranges and greens to begin to appreciate the reds and blues and so forth?

SCG: We certainly can try. Any approach that compares different styles of how people act may help. If you look at trait theory as in Myers Briggs, people can learn to identify with this type or that type and understand other people as very different types from themselves. How can we use this information to get along better with each other or to solve conflicts? Knowing who the other person is does help me to understand and to approach them in a way that's more productive. Otherwise, I just simply state they're wrong or they're benighted. How come they don't see the world the way I see it? That encouragement to learn about differences can sometimes help make things go more smoothly.

RV: You are supporting the notion that one of the things we need to do is develop the healthier aspects of the earlier stages in our systems, even within ourselves. Whether we're orange or green or yellow we can still have access or we are still influenced by the dynamics of those earlier stages.

We need to nurture them in a way that has them shift, becoming constructive processes in our work, in the way we do ourselves in the world. Is that a fair statement?

SCG: I think this is an excellent statement and the focus I tend to put on that when I explain to students or when we work with this material is it's a matter of choice. If you are only red, or only an Opportunist, you really have absolutely no capacity to see anything else. If you're a Diplomat, a real Diplomat, then you have no choice about that behavior. That's just the way you are. That's all you can see. However, if you are at a stage beyond Diplomat, Diplomat responses are part of you and you may have a choice in how to integrate them and how to use them when functional. The amount of choice available is one of the major ways stages differentiate from each other. The higher the stage, the more interpretive and behavioral choices you have.

"...the best approach [to leadership development] is to start with teaching or helping people to become familiar with certain skills rather than talking about theory and stages."

RV: Let's look at the question of lines, the question of whether or not development is all apace, if you will, in the physical, emotional, spiritual, cognitive and other lines of development. Do you see us as potentially at different stages for different aspects (lines) of our being or do we tend to cluster all lines at one stage?

SCG: Another one of the basic controversies.

[Laughter]

William James was the first to talk about the "center of gravity" of our meaning making and if you look at the self as the unit that integrates all the other lines, then I would say we expect some coherence. If you look at separate lines such as the cognitive

or the moral, then I think that if you measured one first and then measured the other there could be real obvious discrepancies. We also generally believe that certain levels of moral development simply are not possible unless you have the cognitive capacity. The cognitive in that way drives a lot of other stuff. I would say you could be cognitively highly evolved and capable of making sophisticated distinctions in a specific arena and applying your sort of smarts to complex problems, but that doesn't mean you are highly evolved and integrated as a person. I have actually observed this on the SCT often enough to have many questions around it.

Approaches to Development

RV: Then in the case of development as an intervention, especially if we're going to talk about leadership development, do you see a strategy, a way of approaching that in business organizations or other contexts? Do you have a methodology that you are leaning towards?

SCG: I wouldn't call it a methodology. It is not that well developed. But I tend to think that the best approach is to start with teaching or helping people to become familiar with certain skills rather than talking about theory and stages. Skills like listening skills and the kind of skills that are described in "emotional intelligence". There are many ways you can help people become alert to some of the differences that are important. Skills like action inquiry and self-reflection can be practiced.

For instance, self-reflection is hard for anybody at the conventional level of development, even Achievers find it hard to deeply self-reflect. Whereas at the post-conventional stages self-reflection becomes just part of who you are. You can't help but to self-reflect. But to teach that, to encourage more people to self-reflect is to give them means, like have them journal about their experiences, do yoga, or teach them other ways of paying attention to themselves that are different from their regular way of operating or running on automatic pilot. These new practices can then get people to a new place or awareness.

I wouldn't introduce developmental theory very early on or I may not introduce it at all. But I would try to get people to start to do little mild meditative things. Try, for example, to introduce a few minutes of silence at the beginning of a meeting and observe how that can change the attention of those present. There are other known ways of how meetings can be done differently than usual. A lot of suggestions and material you can find in [Peter] Senge for instance, in his *The Fifth Discipline Field Book*. There is a lot out there that can be done. These approaches help people to shift from their ordinary, unconscious approaches for holding meetings to a different kind of meeting, even just a tiny bit different so that there's a new expectation.

RV: Is it possible that human systems of organization really emerge from one of the levels, or actually are an accumulation of emergence from different levels as they've developed over time, and that at some point the whole notion of organization, perhaps even the whole notion of business and exchange are transcended so that if you do develop to some point you can no longer authentically participate in some fashion?

SCG: I think it's not that you can't participate authentically but again the choice here is another one as when Torbert talks about Magicians. My sense is that Magicians tend not to be ongoing participants in one organization. They're more the types that would come in from their own free will because they feel they have something unique to contribute or else they are called in as Magicians to do something that the organization on its own capacity cannot do.

It's one thing that I'm sometimes optimistic about and sometimes not. How can we get the whole culture to move to a more diverse, less self-righteous, less rigid perception of things? I imagine a more global society, one where being a global citizen would be the norm. That is a way of looking at oneself as part of humanity rather than seeing oneself as part of a particular group, race, culture,

organization or nation. That's sort of the ideal, the dream many of us have or we wouldn't do this kind of work. But there's also the fact that Western culture is still mostly embedded in the conventional realm. That creates a ceiling or a limit that can be self-reinforcing.

RV: In other words our own personal constructs tend to act as limits or ceilings on our development, on our capacity, on our ability to engage with greater complexity. The same is true of social systems.

SCG: Yes. Social systems are in some ways even more resistant to change, more tending towards the lower common denominator. It's even harder to shift because you have all the people who are really attached to a way of work and life, which may be the only one they know. This accounts for most things in politics. If there's a majority of people who know only their own culture and ideology, then you can imagine how difficult it is to open their minds to other possibilities. Here again I appreciate the beautiful contribution of Spiral Dynamics that makes life circumstances such an important aspect of how we explain all of this. The tendency to go back, to revert to an earlier stage, to simplify things under stress is common not only in individuals, but in systems too.

"I imagine a more global society -- one where being a global citizen would be the norm. That is a way of looking at oneself as part of humanity rather than seeing oneself as part of a particular group, race, culture, organization or nation."

RV: I hear a rumor that you're in the process of writing a book. Is this true?

SCG: A rumor? It is a very difficult process. It's almost two years now since we had a meeting at Ken Wilber's with about 8-10 people trying to get together to write an introductory book about integral leadership. We envision a book that is practical and that would translate complex theories into words that could be read and understood widely without losing the necessary complexity and integrity. Anybody who writes knows that this is one of the most difficult things to do. At what point when you simplify are you actually falsifying what you're meaning? It's just a problem anybody who writes about science knows only too well. And it's a wonderful, wonderful achievement for those few who actually have been able to achieve a popular scientific style.

RV: So I'm unclear by your response whether or not that is really an active project.

SCG: It's an active project. I met last December with John Foreman, the other head writer on the project in Seattle. We really hammered out one chapter and created the whole outline that we think will work for the book. We have a serious beginning and the question is always, since this is voluntary work, when can we carve out some extra time to work on it? But yes, we're going ahead with writing and when we get next together we will make a proposal to the rest of the group and they will help us edit, add ideas, change things.

> *"If you solve a gnarly problem, address a personal conflict or an organizational impasse, if you could look at the four quadrants and how they influence what's going on, you're better off than if you don't, than if you only look at one or the other contributing factor."*

RV: I've noticed, when I look at what people are doing around training programs and work around integral leadership, it seems to me that the emphasis is principally on the individual. There is the use of assessments and interventions that are very individually oriented. Is that what you're seeing as well?

SCG: I do, because it seems unless the individuals in a system have the capacity then really the whole

system cannot move forward. On the other hand, one can say that if you create a particular context for the system then the growth of individual can be supported. This is so often not the case now. Postconventional development is simply not supported in most institutions. A collaborative inquiry organization is very, very rare to be found. There are attempts at creating this type of second tier organization, but it's difficult to sustain them. My hunch is, yes, if we have more people at later stages, then it will also be easier to sustain such organizations.

Integral Leadership

RV: Can you tell me what integral leadership is?

SCG: [Pause – Laughter]

Wonderful question! I have some sense of what I understand it to be. It is leadership that is deeply aware of complexities. It can translate what the agreed upon goals are in such a way that it can appeal to different levels. It offers multiple stories, if you will, about the same goals. Gifted leaders translate what needs to be done into stories that appeal to different people so that, at the end, they can actively engage everybody to take leadership. And again, that is easier said than done and needs a flexible understanding and a dynamic response.

RV: By definition integral leadership is second tier?

SCG: I think so. I do realize that integral has become a catchword as it's being used. You could also say that integral refers to the four quadrants, and then it doesn't necessarily mean second tier. When you teach people at any level to take the four quadrants into account for whatever problem or conflict they're looking at that's another way of defining integral.

RV: What I'm learning from our conversation is we can work with the four quadrants but we can't do AQAL because people at earlier levels or stages such as orange and green, are not going to even be able to see the potential of the second tier.

SCG: That's right. But it's still better to have the four quadrants. If you solve a gnarly problem, address a personal conflict or an organizational impasse, if you could look at the four quadrants and how they influence what's going on, you're better off than if you don't, than if you only look at one or the other contributing factor. Partial analysis is so much what has been done in the past. Even systems theory may only look at the system and not at the individual behavior, not the internal aspect of what is happening. You have models and structures you try to put your own organization into, but I don't think that is enough. Deeper insight and better solutions can be found if you have insight into what is happening in the other quadrants as well and how things are intertwined.

RV: In a sense, Senge's work is integral in that in the **Fifth Discipline** and his subsequent work he attends to both the individual and the system. He addresses the individual in relation to mental models and development through Robert Fritz's work [**The Paths of Least Resistance** and other publications].

SCG: Senge himself is integral, but I think a lot of people have taken the structural, external stuff from him. They just diagram an organization for the cycles that work or don't work. If you only use templates for instance or diagnose "root causes" then you have not fully used what is being offered in Senge's model. That is quite often where systems theory approaches end up.

RV: Are you talking about the system archetypes?

SCG: Yes.

RV: I recently had called to my attention the fact that Ken Wilber has been going through some significant health problems and he seems to be dealing with them with a quality of strength that is really impressive. Is he actively involved in questions of integral leadership at this point?

SCG: My sense from what he has been sending to the Integral Institute members is that he's really focusing on writing out all the things that seem to have been coming through him, very rapidly and in amazing amounts through these last few months of suffering and illness. The new ideas are just so prolific and exciting. He's just trying to keep up writing them down as much as he can and focusing on that.

He is absolutely fantastic. I can't wait to get more segments of the Kosmos trilogy. I really have found his latest writing to be a whole new and exciting integration, different from before, even richer, even deeper, even more differentiated and clear.

RV: Where do you see the work of the Integral Institute, particularly the group that's working on integral leadership, going from here?

SCG: Trying to write. There are two core groups that are writing books. All of the branches are trying to get the integral ideas more into the mainstream. This is really one of the functions we have. We are really trying to overcome the quite enormous hurdles of doing that, with the humility it takes to do it as well.

RV: Who is working with you?

SCG: John Foreman, Steve March and Paul Landraitis are in our group. Also, David Johnson who works with city boards and multiple constituents to change attitudes so that they can construct environmentally-sound cities by creating the necessary policies. Steve McIntosh, the owner and creative director of Zen & Now is on that book project as well. He makes these wonderful Zen clocks, and has an incredible aesthetic sense. His is really the most sophisticated and fine-tuned entrepreneur I have seen in a long time.

RV: Well, is there anything I haven't asked you about that you think would be important for us to include here?

SCG: There's so much.

RV: I know.

SCG: I mean the whole thing about language that's dear to me we haven't addressed. I would also like to do some research that includes comparative measures. You alluded to that earlier; there isn't really much that compares the different measures with each other and that would be interesting.

RV: I hope you get a chance to do that. And where do you go from here, I mean, what's in the future for Susanne?

SCG: Susanne wished she had an academic position and some dedicated graduate students that could work with all the data she has collected over the years and do some interesting things with them that she just doesn't have time for. And I'd love to teach more than I do. Currently, I'm the body at Harthill USA and the company just requires so much administrative attention that I really find myself short on time for doing what I wish to be doing instead: research, creating teaching materials, leading professional workshops, writing the integral leadership book, and more time for just reflecting and sharing ideas.

RV: Susanne, I know we all wish you well in fulfilling those possibilities.

SCG: Thank you.

Integral Executive Education

Leo Burke

RV: What I know of you I think first came out in Ken Wilber's book, *A Theory of Everything*, in which he talked about you as heading up Motorola's leadership development program, is that right?

LB: I was at Motorola for 12 years, the last six of which were in Motorola University. During part of that time, I was Dean and Director of the College of Leadership and Trans-cultural Studies.

RV: That's a big title. Tell us what it means.

LB: At the time Motorola University was organized by colleges in terms of content oriented around different subject areas. One was in software engineering, another in hardware engineering, one in quality, another in sales and marketing. We had one in leadership and trans-cultural studies. The idea for that particular unit was to increase leadership education particularly focused on middle managers and above. There was an added dimension given the global nature of the corporation to increasing trans-cultural literacy among our managers.

RV: Being able to deal with the diversity effectively and actually leverage it?

LB: Yes, absolutely leverage it to understand what the components are that requires it so much more when doing business in Brazil, China or India. We were also interested in the unique characteristics of those cultures that we can incorporate, both with our associates working there in country as well as exporting perspectives to use elsewhere in the world.

RV: What brought you to that position?

LB: Well, I had been doing leadership and organizational effectiveness at Motorola University when we formed those new colleges. It was kind of a natural step for me to start that unit and head it up.

RV: Did you come to the whole area of development and change out of the management role or out of a consulting role?

LB: I had a Master's degree in organization development and had worked as a consultant. I was always in education at Motorola. I started though in engineering education.

RV: Are you an engineer by background?

LB: No, I'm not, but actually that assignment was invaluable to me in terms of understanding our business and where we were going.

RV: Since leaving Motorola you've started an executive program in Integral Leadership?

LB: When I left Motorola I became Associate Dean for Executive Education at the business school at Notre Dame.

RV: When did this executive program on integral leadership begin?

LB: We're just launching it now (2002). We designed it several months ago. The design that we had I would describe as too robust for the market. The design called for a week at Notre Dame, six weeks back on the job with telephone coaching, a lot of assignments and another week at Notre Dame. People thought it was a great idea, but nobody had the time to attend. So we've now condensed it so there's a one week version that we're running in December. It's full, I'll have you know

RV: Congratulations. What was the path that brought you to the concept of integral?

LB: When I was at Motorola U heading up the leadership college in the mid-nineties we had a skunk works projects called the Fayol project, named after Andre Fayol. Fayol's categorization of the functions of management was something that had a lot of staying power for many generations. What would it take to create another breakthrough that would have that level of impact on the thinking about managers and have that kind of staying power? The guiding impetus was two sets of questions. First, what if human beings really aren't who we think they are? Second, what if business really isn't what we think it is?

> *"In my own experience in working with managers at various places around the world of Motorola in China, India and a lot of European states, I found that this whole interior dimension, if it were not fully developed, the ramifications could be disastrous."*

We have these uninspected assumptions of how we plow through our lives and our work. Maybe there's something more here than meets the eye. If we could explore these maybe we could have some insights as to how managers could do their jobs more effectively and serve their constituents by truly adding more value.

I had read some of Ken's work much earlier, but at that time *Sex, Ecology and Spirituality* came out. I was taken with that work and thought that it had significant implications for us. I began passing it around Motorola wherever I could and writing to Ken. At the same time as part of the Fayol Project we were bringing in folks to come to talk to us who

were kind of a little bit off the beaten path for the kinds of people that Motorola would normally be engaging. One was the futurist, Willis Harmon.

RV: One of the founder's of the Institute for Noetic Sciences.

LB: Exactly, and then the co-founder of the World Business Academy. Another was a physicist Dana Zohar who had written *Quantum Society*. Another was a management consultant from India, Debashis Chatterjee, had written a book on Buddhist and Hindu principles of management.

These people would come in and talk to us. We would kick around ideas about where the world was going and how managers needed to develop to be effective in this world. One of the things that struck me was that each of these folks had concluded that the most important thing managers could do was to understand themselves better. That made a real impression on me. They were coming from very different points of view and different educational backgrounds, but they had all reached the same conclusion.

Ken had introduced the quadrants and the holon. It was a very neat, clean notion of the interior dimension that fit with what we were hearing from a variety of other people. Things began to match up.

In my own experience in working with managers at various places around the world of Motorola in China, India and a lot of European states, I found that this whole interior dimension, if it were not fully developed, the ramifications could be disastrous. In fact there is a case study I use now in one of my classes around a famous now fired executive of Motorola who was clearly very brilliant in some respects but didn't have other dimensions of his life together. He led a relatively uninspected life and then created a lot of havoc and damage It cost the company billions of dollars.

RV: This resonates with what's going on for a lot of

financial executives and CEOs these days, doesn't it?

LB: Absolutely. So in early 2000 I was on sabbatical from Motorola and at that time Ken was forming the Integral Institute. We had various pod meetings and I was invited to the first meeting of the business group. After that meeting we formed a small core team that would meet quarterly with Ken and try to flesh out his ideas for applying them to world business. I don't know if you would know all these players, but the guys who are still with this core team, Bob Richards, Fred Kofman, Michael Putz—who's a strategy guy at Cisco—and me.

We continued to meet and work. I found it really stimulating and helpful to attempt to take Ken's work, see how we would apply it in the world of business and how we can make it relevant, practical and tangible. As an outgrowth of those meetings and in my new role at Notre Dame it seemed like just a perfect match to launch something like the executive program. We got it together and we'll see where it goes. Equally exciting is that we are now introducing a one week version of integral leadership into our Executive MBA curriculum.

Integral Leadership

RV: What is integral leadership?

LB: It's thinking in a kind of simplest exposition, taking a look at various dimensions of leadership. This means looking not only at the exterior components of our work life but the inside, or interior, as well. The way we've specifically presented this is to go through not only Ken's notion of quadrants but developmental levels and Ken's treatment of lines of development. These form a pretty coherent picture for people in terms that are sufficiently robust for managers to consider how they both further their own development as well as lead their organizations.

RV: There's an implication in taking this approach that I'd be interested in hearing your ideas about.

I don't think most people in business would have a struggle with the notion of the interior at least in some senses, and the exterior at the individual level. What I find challenging for some, or a different way of thinking about what leadership has to do with the inclusion of the interior or exterior collectives. How do you approach this notion of integral leadership as a phenomenon that is more than an individual phenomenon but is also a collective phenomenon.

"Most business managers really acknowledge the validity of culture even though most don't fully understand it and certainly don't know how to manage or engage it effectively."

LB: The way we've treated it is we've defined the collective exterior as all of the systems and processes that businesses engage and employ. So it's all the stuff you can see when you walk into a factory that's going on, in fact what enabled widgets to be made. The collective interior is culture and shared values. When you look at the collective interior from that point of view, most people get that. Most business managers really acknowledge the validity of culture even though most don't fully understand it and certainly don't know how to manage or engage it effectively. But there's at least the notion that, yes, this is the variable we need to be paying attention to.

One of the exercises used is to see what questions you can ask around each of the four quadrants with regard to a given business issue and the notion that any change initiative that doesn't take all four quadrants into account is likely not going to result in a solution. The quadrants help us see the sets that have some pieces missing.

RV: I think of the holon and the holarchy as a representation literally as a model of everything in the ways that Ken has talked about. Well, if leadership is a phenomenon, at the individual level we can look at values, beliefs, assumptions, aspirations and things like that on the interior as well as individual developmental levels. Then we can look at the behaviors in the upper right related to that. What is the leadership phenomenon in the lower left and lower right quadrants? It's something more specific than culture and shared values, isn't it? It's something more specific than systems and processes?

LB: Clearly our integral business core team acknowledges that that needs to be fleshed out more and I think a lot more work needs to be done there, so I don't have a good answer for you. There clearly are ways a leader engages, leverages, uses, somehow interacts with the collective dimension at various levels within an organization, whether it's within a team, a department, a division or the entire enterprise as an example. But frankly, we have not fleshed that out with the core team, so that's sort of a watch this space. Frankly I think we're talking about a good five-year project that needs to involve lots and lots of people to share enough information. You know, this is where you play a critical role, as sort of a kind of the hub of an information wheel so that practitioners and theorists can learn from each other and flesh these things out more.

RV: One of the things that I think is very interesting about this is the question of how do we begin to make it intelligible to people who are not used to this way of thinking, no matter what quadrant we're talking about. And so there are ways of introducing these ideas and these approaches that are more successful than others. What thoughts have you about that?

LB: The way that we're going is building blocks. You know there's a theory piece people need and then there is obviously practice. The building blocks certainly include a discussion of quadrants. Discussion of quadrants for most people I think has face validity. At least that's what I found in my courses that I've taught to our EMBAs, particularly if it can be framed as a way of looking at how they might think from the point of view of each quadrant as they look at a business issue.

The way we've defined lines of development is we've parsed out six seven lines —a cognitive line, a moral line, an interpersonal line, a physical line, an emotional line, a values line, a spiritual line. When we say physical, we really mean the kinds of decisions you make, interior decisions you make about physical health and well being. When people see that it makes a lot of sense to them. They can understand this, or they've had a boss who was very strong in the cognitive line but a real moron in the interpersonal line. That all makes sense. What it stimulates most people is the interest in horizontal development. One might say, "I haven't been exercising. I need to be thinking about that or cleaning up my diet. Or my interpersonal relationships are not the quality I need them to be. Or the feedback I'm getting suggests that I really need to engage stuff around emotional intelligence."

It doesn't scare people off.

> *"There clearly are ways a leader engages, leverages, uses, somehow interacts with the collective dimension at various levels within an organization, whether it's within a team, a department, a division or the entire enterprise as an example."*

The moral line these days with all this stuff around ethics is sort of a no-brainer. The whole discussion of spiritual is interesting. People find that intriguing. Our approach has been to basically to say, "Do you think this is a legitimate area to talk about? What are your perspectives here?" We point out as Ken does in *Integral Psychology* that there are a lot of ways to define spirituality. When we talk about the levels, that's a little bit trickier.

A Developmental Model

RV: Do you use a particular developmental model?

LB: Well the model that we have, that we started with in our core team, was the Spiral Dynamics®

model. Ken impressed upon us that it's really important to not get into typing people, to say you're an orange, so-and-so is a blue, somebody else is red. The Beck-Cowan-Graves taxonomy applies to the values line and so life is a complex. There are all kinds of different levels for different lines. It's much more complex than just stereotyping somebody, kind of pegging them to a certain point.

In our integral leadership course we use Jenny Wade's terminology, as well as her *Mindsets* instrument. It maps well with Beck since Jenny's work is also based on that of
Clare Graves.

When presenting from an instructional or pedagogical point of view the question always is: Why are you conveying this material? What utility does it have or how does it fit in? I think the justification for presenting something on levels is that it enables people to see the different levels of complexity in a way that they can grasp. They come to appreciate the fact that there are people in their organization at various levels driven by various value sets and interests.

Managing such diverse sets of people is not something you can do with one kind of "fell swoop." It requires much more. It's a more complex task than people might think. People know it's complex at one level because they see that things aren't working the way they think they ought to work. They've just never understood why, and this can provide some kind of insight into the kind of drivers, diverse drivers that people have.

RV: Does it give them anything fresh in the way of tools, strategies or approaches for dealing with that?

LB: For example, Jenny Wade has a very useful workbook. It offers suggestions of how you would lead under certain circumstances, how you would reward people who are coming from different perspectives, how you would design the best job matches. So there are some very practical kinds of suggestions.

We use Wade as the front and then have supplemental material for people that are interested in exploring things. My sense is this is just about enough theory that people are willing to absorb on a first pass here. Especially the folks who are in our population: busy executives. Now they've come away with the notion that there really are these different dimensions: interior, exterior. They hadn't quite thought of it this way before. These lines of development make sense. They can see that. They understand that and say, "These levels are really something. I didn't know that people really go at life quite differently, I get this values level and now I can begin to see that these other levels on these other lines, and…"

RV: And now they're overwhelmed?

LB: Yes, it's a lot. So how do we make that digestible and actionable? The way the device we're using — and there may be ways to do this — is they build a personal action plan of things they want to do differently. And there's a whole lot of other stuff that goes on in this program: 360° feedback and simulation. Also lots of inputs. Fred Kofman does several days in terms of communication, truth telling, emotional intelligence kinds of things. There's also a business issue that threads through the whole week. They engage with looking at a business issue, taking into account the new information that they've gotten at every point.

RV: What would be an example of that?

LB: It can range from "How do I increase market share or introduce a new product into a market?" to "How can I more effectively merge two business operations that are now coming together?" to "How can we more rapidly innovate new product development?" You can really take a range of issues.

RV: Let's look at the implementation, the making it real piece. It sounds like after they're first been introduced to this material they go back home and they have a period of time in which they're receiving coaching, is that correct?

LB: Well, that was true under the original model. Now it'll be a little different with our EMBAs because I have access to them for a longer period of time. But under the new model, they are only with us for a week.

RV: I see, with no follow up.

LB: My experience is the whole follow up process is so challenging in the non-degree world. People just get onto other things. They're just very busy. We'll do some evaluation to see how they are applying and we're trying to figure out. Perhaps there is a pay-per-view service we could offer with regard to follow up that would be of interest to people: either guidance or some kind of coaching. But we have much more to learn there.

RV: And how many people do you have in the program?

LB: The first one we wanted like 25. The first one I think is at 40. [At this time several hundred—5 or 6—have gone through the program with very positive feedback.]

RV: Wow!

LB: Yes. We thought we were getting it right, and then more water came over the dam than we were anticipating. I gave a presentation at the Executive EMBA Council Conference. It was very interesting because these are mostly people that run executive MBA programs. I brought out what we're doing and an overview of an integral model as we're using it with our students, a discussion of quadrants, lines and levels.

I described how we're doing that and then we had a conversation as educators. What should we be doing in executive MBA Programs? Is this legitimate subject matter to be engaging? It was a really interesting set of conversations. The consensus

was that all the emphasis we place on functional and quantitative skills is clearly necessary but not sufficient as we look at the world today. Engaging our students, whether it is through an integral model like we're trying at Notre Dame or something else, is absolutely essential.

And so the reason I'm excited about that is the whole notion that business education, and I think the recent epic scandals can be an accelerant here, is potentially going to renew itself in a way that could be very positive in terms of a much broader view about what it means to be a successful executive or to be an educated MBA.

RV: Have you noticed any fallout from what's been going on with the Enron and post-Enron era in terms of people's openness and receptivity to these ideas?

LB: Yes. I think at Notre Dame there's a self-selection process that goes on with our students, because we're pretty explicit about the fact that one of the things that we offer is an attempt to imbed a discussion around values into most of what we do. This definitely is an area that has the interest of our students. We have a series of CEOs that come in and speak to our students. It has just been very, very interesting in terms of the seriousness with which people are examining these issues. I think there's much more reflection. And, you know, part of it too is given what is going on with the economy, people are coming to the awareness that they're not going to be millionaires in three years. Business really is hard. and do I really want to do this, and...

RV: Maybe I should be a teacher.

LB: Right. We have a huge number of undergrads in Business and I think all because of the run up in the NASDAQ in the nineties. It will be interesting to see the impact of the ethics scandals and the economy. I think the whole thing is for a reduction …

RV: People are starting to question and reexamine, and that can't help but help, you know?

LB: Sure enough.

LB: Exactly.

RV: Well, wonderful, Leo. Thank you so much.

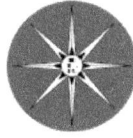

A Developmental Model of Leadership

William "Bill" R. Torbert

RV: I'm really interested in having conversations with people who are doing things that, for me, feed into the idea of an integral approach to leadership. And an integral approach to leadership, it seems to me, is one that is very much concerned with questions of development. And what I'm hoping to do in this interview involves three stages. The first stage is to have you talk a little bit about the role of action inquiry in your work. When I look at materials you have on your web site it is very clear that this has been the heart of your work ever since you were a graduate student. I would like to talk about your perspectives on leadership and leadership development. Third, I'd like you to talk about your current work because you mentioned it has something to do with time, and I'm fascinated to discover what that might be.

BT: Great.

RV: You were a student of Chris Argyris and the whole idea of action inquiry has been central to your work. What is unique about your work in action inquiry?

BT: Although it is definitely true that Chris is a central influence in my life, and that is because he clearly was concerned with putting action and inquiry together, it's also true that at the same time as I met him at Yale I also got to know Bill Coffin, the Yale minister. He's sometimes called the white Martin Luther King, was very involved in the Civil Rights movement, was one of the first Freedom Riders, and later stood in the opposition to the Vietnam War.

There should be a relationship not just between social science theory and professional action, but also between spiritual inquiry and political acts. Chris was relatively conservative, not spiritually oriented and not politically oriented. Bill Coffin was more radically oriented.

And at the same time I was getting to know, not what we think of as philosophy today, but real Socratic inquiry where you are taking action in the conversation and having an influence on one another, almost an alchemical influence. At the same time I found my way into the Gurdjieff Work. This direct spiritual work is a work on attention. Through Plato, Bill Coffin and the Gurdjieff Work, I had a sense that the kind of action inquiry I wanted to do was not only professional in nature, but personal, spiritual and political. It was meant to affect my every waking moment.

All of those were playing a role when I started to inquire further into Yale and the graduate program with Chris Argyris. I took an intervention theory course with him years before he wrote his intervention theory and method book [*Intervention Theory and Method*] and years before he had come up with the name action science. In fact, it was my 1976 book, *Creating a Community of Inquiry*, about the Yale Upward Bound Program that I had founded that first introduced the term action science.

I went into the doctoral program in Individual and Organizational Behavior with the understanding that I could study myself trying to take some action in some way. This turned out to be leading the Yale Upward Bound program: creating it and getting the original grant for it. When it turned out that there was nobody of a proper age to lead it, the Yale people let me do it at the tender age of 22. I was not intervening in a large, Fortune 100 corporation, which was more typical of Chris's work. I was engaged in a very incendiary interracial situation that had a political element to it. It had a profound educational element in it in that the students in my program had never had a good experience in school before. I was working with people who really didn't necessarily share my sense of rationality at all.

Applying An Integral Perspective

RV: What I'm getting as I'm listening to you is already an integral flavor to the way you're engaging with the world or at least with a notion of action inquiry. Not only were you doing an inquiry into the context -- the systems, the environments around you -- but you were also engaged in conscious self-development, a process that could only happen in that context.

BT: Exactly. It seemed to me that the people who ought to be most affected by an action were the initiators of the action. Even though the intent was also to have an influence over somebody else, if you didn't see yourself as learning and transforming through the action, then it seemed to me you were almost certainly off base in a profound way. I'm not coming up with the way in which I knew that at the time except for the fact of all these different influences.

I read Plato's Symposium about Alcibiades who later became the leading general during the Peleponesian Wars. He was the great corporate raider of the third century BC, moving his allegiances back and forth between Athens, Sparta and Persia, trying to create a just environment in a situation in which none of the states seemed just to him. And there he was, as a student of Socrates, saying that only Socrates could make him feel his nothingness. This seems to me to be the place from which all possibility begins -- the meeting of the inner and the outer in the moment

when, listening beyond one's ego, one feels one's nothingness. This is the actual experience of what we're now calling integral.

RV: Was it there in the meetings between Socrates and Alcibiades implicitly or explicitly?

BT: Quite explicitly. Gurdjieff said that the resolution between free will and necessity is that we have the possibility of free will. In ordinary life we don't really exercise free will because we're moved around by all these forces, not just external forces that are studied in social science but psychic, archetypal, cosmic forces as well.

"You can't start out in a pure collaborative mode because, in fact, most people aren't prepared to collaborate. This creates a terrific irony for leadership. It must work toward collaboration or else there isn't significant human development and you don't end up with an effective organization. But you can't mandate collaboration."

RV: I'm reminded of the quote that you have to become somebody before you can become nobody. This speaks to the role of consciousness and awareness before one can become one with God or whatever.

BT: Or Gandhi's now much bandied about phrase "We need to become the change we wish to see in the world."

RV: Yes. And so was that really what you were about as you were doing this Upward Bound work, that you were trying to become the change that you wished to see in the world?

BT: I didn't think those words at that time. But I guess the answer is yes, because first of all I thought it's just too late in world history for another prophet of the future. I have got to do whatever it is I think is right, rather than just write books about it. That

60

was a very important reason for wanting to start the Upward Bound program. I didn't feel very confident. I just knew I couldn't do it any other way.

RV: That reminds me also of a quote from an interview Michael Toms did with Sir Lawrence Vanderpost, about 1994, in England: "At the moment people are saying as if they're bewildered, why haven't we got any great leaders? Why haven't we got another Churchill? Why haven't we got another Roosevelt, or somebody to show us the way?: And he says, "Well it's simply because nature is telling us it's projection. The age of leaders has come and gone. Every person must be his or her own leader now. You must remove your projection and contain the spirit of our time in your own life and your own nature, because to go the old way and follow your leader is a form of psychological imprisonment. We want to be emancipated from that age, and the answer is to profoundly reappraise your realms of government and everything else."

BT: Right. I was very determined when I started Upward Bound to do it in this incredible collaborative way with the staff and not be a traditional leader and so forth. The first week of school we went out to a camp an hour out of New Haven with the students and tried to create the constitution of the school with them. It was chaotic.

RV: In the best sense, perhaps?

BT: That's right, because one of the things I realized afterwards was that we had 60 students and I had learned all the students' names in the first 48 hours. We were all running around trying to get everybody to have a meeting and nobody would go to bed at night and so forth. The outcome was that we all knew each other very well. It did have some positive elements of chaos in it. We did actually create a number of fundamental rules for the school. But these were kids who had never lived a "rule-ly" life in any sense of the word.

We struggled all summer, but we did cut the New Haven high school drop out rate in half the next year for two primary reasons. One, the kids began to have some hope in themselves because somebody cared about them. Two, we learned that most of them needed glasses. They were having a lot of their trouble reading simply because they couldn't see the words, although there were many other problems, too.

RV: In the spirit of the integral perspective what did you learn about yourself in that process?

BT: One of the things that I couldn't understand is why the staff needed so much attention. I thought I was paying them to take care of things. It was completely astonishing to me, but a very important learning. I couldn't take the staff for granted and assume we were all on the same side and were going to the same place or that the kids were the only focus of attention.

As the director, my primary focus needed to be the staff. I needed to create a real team that could work effectively with the students. People told me after my first summer—my best friend told me, "You don't get people's loyalty. You don't understand that you need to befriend the staff, not just the students." I was sort of a beloved fellow but one who was viewed as being completely visionary and not really effective in these incredibly tense circumstances.

The other thing that I learned over two years is that you can't start out in a pure collaborative mode because, in fact, most people aren't prepared to collaborate. This creates a terrific irony for leadership. It must work toward collaboration or else there isn't significant human development and you don't end up with an effective organization. But you can't mandate collaboration.

This gradually led me, as I went to Southern Methodist University after finishing at Yale. I worked with 400 students at a time trying to get them to become entrepreneurs. Of course the students didn't want to do much except drink, go to football games and live on Daddy's money.

We learned to create what I eventually called liberating disciplines. This was a form of organization structure that did give guidance to people, but in such a way that they had to develop skills to guide themselves. The more they developed those skills, the less they got guided. They could work themselves out of being directed by other people if they wanted to. That was my biggest political discovery ever. I have been sort of sad that it hasn't been picked up at all by anybody else, because in a way I think I actually figured out how to do Marx's Dictatorship of the Proletariat in a way that would end up with liberation rather than tyranny.

Stages of Development

RV: It sounds like you've laid the foundation for a developmental perspective in suggesting that there are stages, layers, needing to be established in order for higher levels or layers to thrive.

BT: Right. I first discovered that, by looking back at the Upward Bound program and seeing stages in the organization's development. Only after working out a theory of that did I come back and see that, of course, most of the theory that already existed was about individual development. They were really parallel. Both things are true. This eventually leads one to the idea that the notion of timing is critical to effective action, because you have to have a sense of the developmental logic of the systems, of the people and of yourself. That will determine what's right about the leadership action at a particular time, rather than some ideology that tells you what's right at all times.

RV: I noticed in your 1993 book, *Sources of Excellence*, you are focusing on business leadership. What was it about business leadership or organizational leadership that attracted you?

BT: When I got here to Boston College as Dean of the MBA program, I realized that I was engaged in a traditional leadership function. At the same time we were trying to educate leaders. At that point I began to look at business leadership and political leadership in a more disciplined way than I had before. But it 's hard to say exactly when it began because in a way it goes back right to Bill Coffin. I was excited by him, because he was a leader who was both intellectual and practical.

My 1991 book, *The Power of Balance*, has a whole chapter on philosopher kings and queens. I discuss six contemporary leaders, most of whom are not that well known and who exhibited a capacity for developmental leadership and effect. The 1987 book, *Managing the Corporate Dream*, is also heavily focused on business leadership.

"A great upstream leader is one who re-galvanizes people's vision and questions the way in which they have been seeing things."

RV: *In Sources of Excellence* you indicate that you were doing what you called "a highly critical re-reading of modern history and economic theory from a perspective that speaks about and attempts to illustrate an unusual process of upstream leadership that is set properly to complement productive, goal-oriented downstream leadership." Could you say something about this concept?

BT: The ultimate idea about action inquiry is to be both in action and inquiry at the same time. Our attention normally runs downstream. We're attracted to a topic for some reason or other, maybe because of our own intention. It passes through our thought, into words and gestures and out to another person. That's the way attention normally flows. I call that the downstream flow of attention. The upstream flow is back from "What am I seeing," "What kind of reaction am I getting from the outside world." Are my actions in fact appropriate and having the influence I intend them to? I first question whether my performance at the bodily visible level is adequate. I might change that. That would be single loop learning.

At the same time the response questions my overall structure or strategy, my action logic. I may need to do some double loop learning and change the way

I'm going about this whole thing or what I imagine is really happening. Then, finally, if I'm open enough to it, there could be a question that flows all the way back. This is triple loop feedback that goes back to the way I'm attending in the first place. That's the upstream direction. A great upstream leader is one who re-galvanizes people's vision and questions the way in which they have been seeing things. George Washington and Abraham Lincoln are the two great Presidents for creating the vision of union and recreating the vision of union in the midst of action.

Meaning and Identity

RV: By moving into triple loop learning, aren't you getting into the question of meaning and identity?

BT: Absolutely. I think both double loop and triple loop do. I see any developmental transformation as a double loop change. The action logic of the person or the system changes. And in your early action logic is your identity. It's the quality of the later action logics that they recognize that any particular structure I'm working in isn't necessarily my identity. My identity is actually in the ongoing action and inquiry into a particular action logic.

RV: When you speak of action logic what model are you referring to?

BT: It's the phrase that I've come to use for what other people call developmental stages. I think the notion of stages is very abstract and raises all sorts of problems about it, especially at the later developmental action logics. The latest action logics aren't stage-like in their nature. They don't capture you in the way the earlier ones do. In [Robert] Kegan's notion of subject and object, in each movement towards a later developmental position you take the action logic you were formerly subject to and turn it into object. You manipulate it by yourself. This moves us to a place where we can be so alert and awake that we recognize that our every thought is simply an expression of a particular action logic. We're not caught by any

of our action logics or we're caught for shorter periods of time. We're able to swim back upstream again. We experience that part of the problem we just created was by getting identified or stuck in a particular action logic.

RV: In the book that you co-wrote, ***Personal and Organisational Transformations***, what I might have thought of as stages, like Opportunist, Diplomat, Expert, Achiever, Individualist, Strategist, Magician, these are all different kinds of action logics?

BT: Yes, I like this theme a lot better. A lot of the earlier works have words like stages, but that's what I mean. In my understanding of each of these action logics, they aren't simply mental logics. They encompass your action repertory and, at the same time, limit or widen it, depending on the quality of the action logic.

RV: What is the relationship between action logics and vMemes in Spiral Dynamics®?

BT: I think there's a close relationship. I think we're looking at the same phenomena and seeing them very nearly the same.

RV: Is there something that differentiates this work from Spiral Dynamics®?

BT: We're gradually exploring that through people like Susanne Cook-Greuter, who is really looking at the way they work methodologically. I've read some of the stuff. I'm unable to find the real core of the research base of it, even though I've looked a bit. I've looked at some stuff about the original work and it's just hard to find the original data, but when I read about the different colors, they're similar in some ways and different in some ways.

Don Beck and Jenny Wade are both now talking about there being two ways of moving from the conventional to the post-conventional: an adaptation of the feminist work on individual achievement vs. a more communal orientation. I haven't been able to find empirical support for that myself. In my work it seems that it is progressive. What I call the Expert is the more tightly bound, more archetypically masculine perspective. The Achiever is a slightly more feminine, relational position. They have their sequence working a little bit differently at that point. Their blue seems to me to be very, very, very close to my Diplomat. Green seems to be very close to what we are now calling the Individualist, the position in between Achiever and Strategist that we hadn't differentiated for a long time, even though it can be differentiated in the scoring system.

RV: In the book you actually link them together.

BT: Yes. We're doing another edition and we're going to break out the Individualist some more along with the parallel organizational stage that we'll probably call the Social Network.

RV: We're bandying around a couple of terms that I want to check to see what the quality of meaning is for you. The two terms are leader and leadership. What is the relationship between those two terms in your mind? Are they the same? Is one just the larger picture of the other or what?

BT: First, I think it is good to separate the notion of leader or leadership from any particular role in an organization. A CEO may or may not function actually as a leader. There has been a lot of discussion of the distinction between management and leadership or a manager and a leader. An Achiever can be an effective manager and a Strategist can be an effective leader. A Strategist in any position in an organization is likely to take leadership. And a Strategist is also someone who recognizes that you don't want to isolate leadership in a single person, so the Strategist will tend to try to create a collaborative situation in which multiple people can exercise leadership, whatever their formal position. By contrast, an Achiever and the earlier action logics will tend to see leadership more hierarchically and will tend to identify themselves as the leader in an exclusive way rather than as a leader who can facilitate more general leadership.

RV: There may be a pattern of meaning associated with leadership at each of the action logics.

BT: Oh, definitely, that's right! I do think that. One of the sentence stems we added to the Loevinger Sentence Completion Test, because there were no sentences relating to managers, is a sentence stem which says, "A good boss …" It would be fascinating to do an article just on what Diplomats say about the boss compared to what Experts say vs. what Achievers and Strategists say. One of the things you find is that at the later action-logics, people don't like the notion of boss. And so they'll often pick an argument with the beginning of the sentence stem.

"I think it is good to separate the notion of leader or leadership from any particular role in an organization. A CEO may or may not function actually as a leader."

RV: I remember when I did it I think my response was something very brief, something like, "A good boss is no boss." What have you learned about the performance of CEO's looking through these lenses?

BT: I think they are the vortex of the paradox of leadership. Given what I've learned, I believe that the CEO is tremendously important because there are people of all action logics in his or her organization. It's not going to cut the mustard to simply be lovey-dovey and advocate collaboration. It just isn't enough.

There are emergencies and there are times when the CEO has to put their ass on the line, partly because other people won't do it and partly because people are projecting their needs for leadership onto the CEO. There is this constant movement back and forth between performing in a way that earlier stage people will recognize as leadership and performing in a way that gradually involves the entire organizational system so that the members of the organization evolve out of those early action logics.

I remember when I came here and wanted to lead a major change in the MBA curriculum (which eventually turned the curriculum into an action oriented one rather than merely a bunch of separate courses and separate disciplines). I had no credibility at the outset. One of the first things I did was unilaterally send out a memo saying, "It has come to my attention that professors fail students in courses and then change the failure later to an Incomplete by allowing the student to do something more in order not to get a failure." I said, "It's perfectly legitimate to give somebody an Incomplete when you have negotiated with the student and they can't finish the course and you agree that they will do something after it's over. You hand in your Incomplete and when they finish you change the grade. There is a grade change form for that. But if a student has simply failed and has failed to make an agreement with you about how to complete the course, then that's a Failure. There will no longer be any changes of failures into Incompletes."

I was only reasserting a University policy, but I did it unilaterally. It was no nonsense. There is a bottom line here in terms of basic quality. It made people respect me; it was little things like that. And then we had a big emergency. I had my first student meeting when I was hoping to make friends with the students and get to know people. I had come in the middle of a semester and they virtually had placards out denouncing one particular teacher from a minority population. The teacher was just really fundamentally inadequate, but once a person is teaching a course you can't usually change them during the course.

Through a series of conversations he agreed to step down and somebody else volunteered to step in. In three days I had gotten a change in the teacher through a completely consultative and collaborative process, but still, completely led by me. Those early incidents began to give people confidence

that I would take action in real cases for relatively just outcomes and that I couldn't be pushed around too much. Slowly, slowly over the next year we developed a collaborative team that eventually persuaded the faculty to pass this curriculum.

CEO Performance

RV: All of this has led to some findings as you've applied these to doing your research. You've actually had some findings about CEO performance. Could you summarize those?

BT: Well, the findings we're talking about right now come from a post hoc study. Several of my collaborators, including the Harthill group in England—David Rooke is my co-author on the main study—and I had done a number of consulting engagements, many of them over a period of several years. We were interested in seeing whether we could help organizations transform more than once. Of course, these were all cases in which we had been invited in by somebody, not always at the initiative of the CEO. Sometimes it would be somebody else in the organization who took the initiative, usually somebody at the vice-presidential level. In a number of cases, it was the CEO.

Just the fact that they were interested in this kind of work indicated that, on average, they might be a slightly later action logic than you'd expect to find in the general population. We did ask them, on a voluntary basis, if they and their senior teams would like to get feedback on the sentence completion tests. So all the CEO's and most of the members of their teams took these and received feedback on them.

What we found was that half of the CEO's measured at the Strategist stage. This is characterized as more mutually oriented and more timing oriented. It is more oriented towards action inquiry without necessarily knowing the word, but just more able to do first and second person inquiry as well as more formal third person inquiry, say about their competitive situation.

Half of the CEO's were at an earlier action logic: one Diplomat, two Experts and two Achievers. After several years we felt quite effective with them, but we realized when we started to talk about it that there were several cases where we had not been effective. We decided to do a study of it.

We got three of us who had been deeply involved to identify the organizational stages, which had never been quantified before. We had paragraph descriptions of them as well as quite a few case illustrations. We all knew these ten cases that we had been involved with quite well. Three of us each independently tried to use our knowledge of the organizational stage theory to make judgments about whether they had transformed or not, and how much.

We were first of all delighted to discover that we had very high reliability on the findings and basically agreed on all ten cases. In one case we had a disagreement about just how many transformations had occurred. So we had a more than .9 reliability on that. What we found was that all five of the CEO's who were at the Strategist action logic had been associated with successful transformations, on average two successful transformations. All the cases where there was no transformation, and the one case in which there was regression, were associated with CEO's who were at earlier action logics than the Strategist.

Another interesting point we didn't make in the article was that all the consultants measured at the Strategist or later than Strategist logic. The one who measured at a later than Strategist action logic was the only one who was associated with CEOs who were not yet Strategists but who nevertheless supported organizational transformation with the help of the consultant. That seems to suggest that perhaps a very late action-logic consultant can actually bridge the dilemma of a CEO who really isn't up to fully modeling the collaborative role. Somehow, this consultant can influence that CEO to get involved in changes that permit other people

to start developing in the organization. But that was just one consultant and two CEOs. This doesn't have a lot of weight as a quantitative finding.

"The bottom line, the position in the industry and the reputation of the company all changed very, very positively for the companies that had positive transformations."

RV: Was there any link between these transformations and the bottom line for these companies?

BT: Oh, absolutely! We studied that separately. The bottom line, the position in the industry and the reputation of the company all changed very, very positively for the companies that had positive transformations. The two that simply didn't transform were more or less treading water and may be slightly worse off at the end in terms of bottom line and industry standing. The one that regressed experienced tremendous negative effects on industry position and even some ethical issues. In that one, by the way, the consultant resigned from the job because of the repeated incapacity to have any influence. In the end the CEO resigned.

Intervention Methodologies

RV: Was there comparability of intervention methodologies across the cases?

BT: In a general there was a strong comparability. I've just done another sort of analysis of this where I now have this model of 27 different types of action research. I've been counting up how many different kinds of action research get used in different cases, and I applied this to the earlier study of the ten organizations. There wasn't any kind of precise comparability because the methods really were tailor made for each separate situation. However, always a part of the intervention at some point would be to try to develop a culture where every meeting at the senior management level had all members of the meeting exercising the leadership role (as they became adept with this they would take this approach to their subordinates and so on down). This goes back to our question of leadership. We were really trying to develop a distributed sense of leadership in a formal way. We created five or six or seven different leadership roles and then they would get gradually rotated around the team over a period of several years.

RV: You would have a rotating Chair at the meeting, for example, and things like that.

BT: Exactly right! You'd have the meeting Chair, the agenda creator, the process manager, the assessment person who would provide at the end of the meeting a little instrument or a little five minute debriefing. You'd have somebody in charge of projects that were supposed to be completed by the team in between meetings. This would smarten things up and get people feeling like you got results from meetings. People got a lot of feedback about their leadership capacities. That's just one of a dozen or more types of action research that were conducted in each organization. Participation in taking the sentence completion tests and receiving feedback was a common one, and so on.

> *"A timely performance is an artistic performance. It can't be generated by rules. It can't be generated by generalizations. It has to be mediated by an awareness that is connected to movement in the moment."*

RV: Are there any kind of guiding principles of what effective leadership is or what organizations need to do to develop leadership?

BT: In *Sources of Excellence* I say there are four leadership virtues. They correspond to this notion of four territories of reality: the outside world, one's own performance, one's action logic and the capacity for attention or vision. Visioning is one of the leadership virtues. That's obviously not particular to me. A lot of people have said it, but I'm talking about generating increasingly wide and deep visioning throughout a family, organization or society that goes beyond quantitative development (e.g., larger market share) to include qualitative development (e.g. a triple bottom line that integrates environmental, social, and economic sustainability).

The second virtue I call empowering, which is also no new thing but it doesn't just mean empowering other people. I speak of it as exercising power in an appropriately vulnerable, mutuality enhancing, transforming way.

The third leadership virtue I call timing. I speak of artistry in action – performance that weaves together the immediate, the long term and the eternal.

RV: That's beautiful. And the fourth?

BT: The fourth virtue I call schooling. Creating learning organizations where adults simultaneously learn and produce.

The Artistic Perspective

RV: There are two things that I really wanted to have you comment on before we're through. One is it seems to me that there is really a quality of the artistic in what you're doing with action inquiry because you not only do the academic thing, but you also seem to include other kinds of models and perspectives—poetry and art, for example. Will you talk about that? And then I would like to go on and get into the timing piece a little bit.

BT: They're not disconnected. A timely performance is an artistic performance. It can't be generated by rules. It can't be generated by generalizations. It has to be mediated by an awareness that is connected to movement in the moment. *Sources of Excellence* is a series of lectures. It was a live performance. In the middle of the book is a series of pieces of art that I displayed at the lectures. I was trying to embody the ideas, not just talk about them.

Before I came to Boston College I spent two years creating another organization called the Theater of Inquiry. That was meant to help me develop my capacities for artistic performance and at the same time create an environment that really raised a question with people as to what they ought to be doing at each moment. That created a frame that was not a frame. It was a frame that could not be taken for granted in various activities. But there were various different activities, an Action Workshop in which when you came into the room you didn't know whether you were supposed to sit or stand. I wanted to introduce people to keeping an ongoing upstream questioning alive at the same time as achieving downstream results.

RV: It sounds like method acting.

BT: It had a relation to that, I suppose. We had another activity called The Business School for people who wanted to start their own businesses. We started our own business as a way of teaching people how to start a business. Another kind of activity was a series of public performances in which the first act was a presentation to the audience, sometimes by several actors as well as me. Then the second act was a series of exercises performed with the audience. The third act was a conversation about what the hell all of this meant. Each one was a rather tense event because each one was totally unique. There was an effort not to create a coercive environment for the audience. It was an intense developmental event because audiences come expecting to be entertained relatively passively. We transformed that expectation. There had been this group called the Living Theater in the late sixties and early seventies that sort of attacked audiences, exposed themselves and forced them to do things. I said, "No, that's not the kind of leadership that I want to model or that I want to generate." I was searching around for how to do this.

RV: Where did you do this?

BT: It was here in Boston. I had come back from California. I had twin sons and I didn't have a job at the time. Luckily I eventually got this Graduate Deanship at BC. In the meantime I made a little money doing this other thing. The theater performances were at the Harvard School

of Education in their nice Longfellow Hall. I had a sculptor friend who let me use his studio for my action workshops. I begged, borrowed and stole basically.

RV: You were very much being an entrepreneur.

BT: Well, yes, and not a very successful one from an economic point of view, but we survived.

"I think first of all that all of our life and with all of our knowledge, if we understood it correctly we 'd be aiming toward the present moment instead of trying to have absolute certainty about the whole world."

RV: From what I understand about entrepreneurs it takes them about eight tries or more to be able to be successful.

BT: That's right. My next entrepreneurial role was as a pagan Graduate Dean in a Jesuit graduate school.

RV: Wonderful.

BT: It worked better that time. I've been at BC for 23 years.

The Subect of Time

RV: Great. So then what is this about time? I know you were just doing a workshop in England. You were talking about doing something around time while you were there, and you've brought up the subject of timing a couple of times during this conversation.

BT: We had a wonderful seminar in England, at Bath, with their Center for Action Research and Professional Practice that Peter Reason and Judy Marshall direct. Peter is one of the co-authors of the *Handbook of Action Research*, which came out two years ago. He and Judy Marshall have been wonderful collaborators with me, with one another, with their students and with a lot of other people over the years. He is a wonderful person who brings people from different disciplines together. "Cooperative inquiry" is one of his phrases and "participatory world view" is one of his concerns. But in any event, I raised a question with the 30 people who were there: "Let's have each of us think about an occasion when we think we exercised timely action, or an occasion that is upcoming when we desperately want to be timely. What does it mean?"

We had a great conversation about why I care about it so much. Well, because I think first of all that with all of our life and with all of our knowledge, if we understood it correctly we 'd be aiming toward the present moment instead of trying to have absolute certainty about the whole world. What we would want is to be wakeful and attuned to the present situation and provide the best leadership we possibly can in it. That kind of knowledge isn't a "Well, this is the answer to everything" kind of knowledge. It is a live inquiry in the moment. I understand that we're trying to create a greater intensity of action inquiry in each moment rather than a greater certainty that will cover all moments.

RV: I understand that from the point of view of awareness, consciousness and development that we can only take action and be powerful in the moment. However, we can have intuition, imagination, and so forth. That allows us to tentatively anticipate the future as well as to learn from the past. So there is a role for memory, as distorted as it may be, as well as a role for intuition.

BT: Absolutely, but their role is to aim toward the present. We want to remember the past for the purpose of seeing the patterns leading up to the present moment, that is, what kind of pattern we're performing in, what game we're playing now, actually. We want to bring a new possibility to life in this moment based on what we want for the future.

RV: Our aspirations.

BT: Based on our aspirations or our intentions. This idea of 27 different kinds of action research is that there are nine kinds of research in the past, nine in the present and nine in the future, but they all come back into the present which is at the center of it. We want to know our intentions for the future in order to know how to act now.

Consciousness

RV: I've heard Fred Kofman say something to the effect that consciousness is a critical business skill and it sounds like you're saying something like that.

BT: One doesn't know what one is doing without it. One doesn't know how far one is from knowing what one is doing without it. One must be conscious of how limited one's awareness is in order to inquire deeply enough in the present, in order to find out what needs doing. What's the priority?

RV: You had this dialogue about time and orientation to time in England. What was your take away from that experience?

BT: I'll get a chance to really find out what my take away was when I get on my email, because I invited them all to write up their experiences. Then I will share the data with everybody in the place. There was a videotape of the event and I guess a transcription will be made of it. In some ways I haven't even begun to assess the take away. We really engaged the questions that you and I have just opened up here about the past and the future and the present and how they relate to one another. We also discussed how some of the women were arguing that by stressing intention I was occluding attention, and that attention is receptive and intention is projecting and that I was being too masculine.

I certainly didn't disagree with the point. The need to awaken a finer and deeper attention is a critical need, and part of what that attention is for is to determine one's own intention. My notion is that these three qualities of time that we call past, present and future, really are three distinct dimensions. When we talk about past we're really talking about the durational quality of time or the linear quality of time.

When we're talking about the present, we're talking about a dimension orthogonal to linear time, the eternal now. It's not a quality that we experience all the time. Most of the time we're not even aware we're in the present, we're not aware that we can cultivate the experience of duration and the experience of the eternal now through an active listening.

The third dimension of time, the future, is the volume of all possibilities. To research the future I have to research the volume of possibilities. That means I have to get outside any limiting frames based on my past. This is a daunting notion.

Action Logic Challenges

RV: Is there a challenge at each of those different action logics around each of those three?

BT: What happens up until the Strategist stage is that people take their action logic frames for granted as the very nature of reality itself. They may have moments of experience that could be named "eternal now," but they don't know what to make of them, they don't know anything about cultivating them particularly, and they don't even have a sense of the importance of duration. Most people's thought is categorical in the sense that there are some things that are always right to do and some things that are always wrong to do. The notion that there is something right for a particular time is a notion that only begins at the Strategist stage. That's when people become interested in history, the things that lead us to think the way we do now, lead our families to be the way they are, or lead our country to be the way it is. A really serious thought about that affects the person thinking, his or her own life and destiny. It affects professional thinking about history, which of course anybody at any stage could do. It is only at the later action logics that time becomes more important than space, that mind becomes more

important than matter. At the earlier stages matter is felt to be more significant than time. What already exists determines what is going to be.

RV: That brings me to what may be our closing notion. That has to do with the question of development itself. Do you see people actually moving between these action logics in a lifetime? Do people who are Achievers, for example, become Individualists? Do Individualists become Strategists, and so forth? Or is that really something that is quite difficult to do?

"You have to get engaged in some kind of second person discipline where it really counts—some kind of dialogue or team that's really trying to do something, where there are real problems and you have to try to bring your first person research, your meditation or martial art, to the second person setting."

BT: It's certainly difficult to do. In the general populations that we've measured the modal stage is the Expert stage. This implies that for most people most development stops after high school. Most people never do make another developmental transformation

On the other hand, we've measured people who have made developmental transformations and I know their stories because I've known them well for years. I have seen people move from one stage to another over a period of time. When I was a Dean at BC and running the action effectiveness program we would take the top 10-12 students each year (the best students would apply for it) and make them consultants to the next year's first-year students. The first-year students would work in teams and would have to do various things together, each person taking different leadership roles, etc.

The people who volunteered for the consulting role went through a really intense process over both years. Almost 100% of them transformed from one action-logic to another, although almost none of the other students in the MBA program did. Our first year program, part of whose point was to help people transform, wasn't powerful enough. It took the second year and the sort of minority who were intrigued enough and already moved enough by the process to want to engage in it more. They did transform, for the most part.

For years we had an alumni group that wanted to continue working together. It was made up almost entirely of people who had been in this consulting role. Again, we found that over a 3-5 year period a number of them transformed according to the measure and according to our experience of them.

RV: I have a hypothesis that probably most of the people who are reading this are going to be either Experts, Achievers or Individualists, with maybe some Strategists and Magicians thrown in, and if there's an Ironist out there I want to know who it is.

BT: They won't tell you.

RV: They won't tell me, right. For those Achievers and Individualists who aspire to some of these lofty heights, do you have any advice for them?

BT: I do think it is tremendously helpful to become familiar with this theory, because it does lay out some of the markings of a path that seems to be consistent across religious traditions and so forth. There is a path and knowing a little bit about it helps. But then, you know you can't just read books and you can't just go to groups and talk about it. You have to engage in first person and second person research. You have to get engaged in some kind of personal discipline: meditative, martial arts. You have to get engaged in some kind of second person discipline where it really counts—some kind of dialogue or team that's really trying to do something, where there are real problems and you have to try to bring your first person research, your meditation or martial art, to the second person

setting. You have to be trying to do the three types of research, first, second and third person, subjective, intersubjective, and objective research. You have to be trying to do them. Not everybody does it by being a social scientist obviously. Some people do them through the crafts and the arts, dancing and theater.

RV: Is there anything that either you have published or that you would recommend that someone look at that describes this in more detail?

BT: There's huge numbers of things on the practice of development. Anybody who is reading your stuff knows the major authors of developmental theory, at least the contemporary ones.

It is very important to find an oral tradition, to find mentors as you read about developmental theory. As you read about late action-logic leaders in The Power of Balance (which is out of print, but available by e-mailing me), ask yourself whom you know who seems late stage. Students will write about a leader in the company and say, "I see him every now and then and he's just like you described the Strategist." They give a very convincing description of how this person acts in meetings and so forth. I say, "Go and ask that person to be your mentor." That sort of person loves that request even though they are very busy and probably three ranks above you. "Go and ask them." Well, most people never get up the guts to do it. But to me that' s been the key for me. I went to these people who were way beyond me, Bill Coffin and Chris Argyris. And I just got engaged with them. I think that's an important thing for people to do.

RV: Having that leader in a developmental sense in our own lives is really important. It's like taking leadership in your own life. You do it in relation to a leader who has demonstrated already how to do it.

BT: When I got to be 21, I thought that I now needed 21 years of adult education.

RV: Is there anything I haven't asked you that you

wish I had?

BT: Well, it's wonderful, you know, you're such a great interviewer. You can see I just go wild and I expect you to rein me in. I've loved how you have managed to stay on point and weave a pattern into the conversation as I go wild. I just want to really

appreciate how much fun this has been.

NOTES

There are references to holons and quadrants. Briefly, a holon is a whole that is also part of something else. Virtually everything can be thought of using the "map" of a holon. Here is such a map:

	Internal	**External**
Individual	Values, beliefs, assumptions, knowledge, worldview, intentions	Behavior, biology
Collective	Culture, shared values, implicit social agreements	Systems, processes, structures, technology

In addition, there are references to Spiral Dynamics®. That copyrighted material is not reproduced here without permission. However, we can provide a summary guide:

First Tier:
    (1) Beige: Survival/Self
    (2) Purple: Magic/Tribes
    (3) Red: Control/Self
    (4) Blue: Right and Wrong/Community
    (5) Orange: Achievement/Self
    (6) Green: Equality/World
Second Tier:
    (7) Yellow: Integrative/Self
    (8) Turquoise: Holism/Universe
    (9) Coral...

A key distinction between first and second tier is that when we are centered in one of the levels of first tier, we are at odds with other levels, while in second tier we can communicate effectively with all first tier levels.

*A great deal more discussion of these models may be found in the pages of the **Integral Leadership Review**: http://www.integralleadershipreview.com.*

Questions for Exploration

1. How would you describe each conversant's view of leadership. Do they define it?

2. Do they distinguish between the concept of leader and the concept of leadership?

3. How do they see the relationship between leading and the context: culture and systems?

4. What is the relationship between leader and follower?

5. Why is distributed leadership important?

6. What common themes can you find in the conversations/

7. What is the relationship between leadership and change?

8. What is the relationship between leading and managing?

9. How are things different in business vs. government or not-for-profit? How are they the same?

10. What are the critical elements for developing leaders?

11. How are stages of development relevant to leadership?

12. What is required to develop vertically, horizontally?

Bibliography

Selected Books by the Conversants

Riane Eisler

Educating for a Culture of Peace, with Ron Miller. Portsmouth, NH: Heinemann, 2004.

Sacred Pleasure: Sex, Myth, and the politics of the Body—New Paths to Power and Love. San Francisco: HarperCollins, 1996.

The Chalice and the Blade: Our History, Our Future. New York: HarperCollins, 1987.

The Gate: A Memoir of Love and Reflection. Lincoln, NE: iUniverse, 1999,

The Partnership Way: New Tools for Living and Learning, (with David Loye). Brandon, VT: Holistic Education Press,

The Power of Partnership: Seven Relationships That Will Change Your Life. Novato, CA: New Wprd Library, 2003.

The Real Wealth of Nations. San Francisco: Berrett-Koehler Publishers, Inc., 2007.

Tomorrow's Children: A Blueprint for Partnership Education in the 21st Century. Boulder, CO: Westview Press, 2000.

Fred Kofman

Conscious Business: How to Build Value Through Values. Boulder, CO: Sounds True, 2006.

Susanne Cook-Greuter

Creativity, Spirituality and Transcendence: Paths to Integrity and Wisdom in the mature Self. Amsterdam: Elsevier Press, 1999.

Transcendence and Mature Though in Adulthood. Lanham, MD: Rowman & Littlefield, 1994.

William R. Torbert

Action Inquiry: The Secret of Timely and Transforming Leadership. San Francisco: Berrett-Koehler, 2004.

Managing the Corporate Dream: Restructuring for Long-term Success. np/d

Personal and Organisational Transformations: through action inquiry., with Dalmar Fisher and David Rooke. Boston: Edge\Work Press, 2001.

Sources of Excellence: An Unorthodox Inquiry into Quality. Boston: Edge\Work Press, 1993.

Additional Resources

The following publications are referred to or carry information useful to extending your understanding of these conversations:

Don Edward Beck and Christopher C, Cowen. **Spiral Dynamics: Mastering Values, Leadership, and Change**. Malden, MA, USJR: Blackwell Publishers, 1996.

Frank Visser. **Ken Wilber: Thought as Passion**. Albany, NY, USJR: State University of New York Press, 2003.

Jenny Wade. *Changes of Mind: A Holonomic Theory of the Evolution of Consciousness.* Albany: NY: State University of New York Press, 1996.

Ken Wilber. **A Theory of Everything**. Bost 1996.on: Shambhala Press, 2000.

Ken Wilber. **Integral Psychology**. Boston: Shambhala Press, 2000.

Ken Wilber. **Instegral Spirituality**. Boston: Integral Books, Shambhala Press, 2006.

Additional Volumes in This Series

Volume 1: Research and Theory (2007)

Volume 3: CEOs on Leadership (To be released 2008)

Volume 4: Coaches and Consultants (To be released 2008)

How you can purchase these volumes:

**http://www.integralleadershipreview.com/store
or contact
russ@integralleadershipreview.com**

www.ingramcontent.com/pod-product-compliance
Lightning Source LLC
Chambersburg PA
CBHW051231200326
41519CB00025B/7332